MOVING ON...

Karen Stockdale Sandvig

CompCare®
Publishers

Library of Congress Cataloging-in-Publication Data
Sandvig, Karen J., 1956–
        Moving on: leaving dysfunction behind to restore and renew
        relationships/Karen Stockdale Sandvig.
            p.cm.
ISBN 0-89638-359-8

1. Adjustment (Psychology) 2. Self-actualization (Psychology) 3. Interpersonal
relations 4. Change (Psychology) I. Title.
BF335.S16   1993   93-24593

Cover design by Chris Garborg
Edit and interior design by Leah Peterson

Inquiries, orders, and catalog requests should be addressed to
CompCare Publishers
3850 Annapolis Lane, Suite 100
Minneapolis, MN 55447
Call 612/559-4800
or toll free 800/328-3330

To my parents, Marvin and Marlene Stockdale, who loved me enough to let me go. Through their courage, strength, faith, care, and guidance, I have seen that reality works. They show me, by example, that maintaining a healthy, positive attitude is a lifelong process and that leaving dysfunction behind means never giving up on the tremendous power of love.

CONTENTS

PART III: KIDS—THE INSULATED CIRCLES

PART IV: EXTENDED FAMILY—THE OUTER CIRCLES

FOREWORD

by Judi Bumstead, M.A., MFCC

Codependent. Adult child. Inner child. Dysfunctional family. Infamous terminology from the '80s. The concepts are still very applicable and useful to help us continue personal growth and healing. But the words themselves may not serve us as well as they once did. Many of them have reached the point of saturation. We are tired of being put in "boxes with labels."

In *Moving On*, Karen Stockdale Sandvig takes the labels off, unwraps the packages, and focuses on helping people get on with their lives. She stays away from confusing psychobabble and uses buzz words only to capture the meanings of things we need to know. She has created a solid bridge between the painful wrenching often experienced in the past and the continued healing and hope necessary for the future.

Karen offers systematic, practical guidance. Her genuineness and passion for positive living shine through her words. She lives what she writes and offers both advice and activities that she uses for herself. Everyone can benefit from *Moving On*.

As a therapist, I recommend it to my clients. Please don't fail to follow through on the exercises and suggestions. This is where your own heal-ing will be furthered. We have much knowledge in our world today, but, as Karen suggests, we still need to move on to healthy, more positive lives and to put what we know into practice.

May God bless you on your journey as you move on with your life!

ACKNOWLEDGMENTS

Acknowledging those who help and support us on our journeys to positive, healthy lifestyles is an important, albeit small, way to thank those who have contributed to who we are today and who we will become tomorrow.

My love and commitment I give to my husband, Douglas, and our two sons, Matthew and Lucian. Moving on together in the circles of our lives is not always easy, but it is a gift and a privilege that I would not trade for anything in this world.

My heart and my deep gratitude I give to my friends, the "Scooter Crew," for loving me enough to help me birth this book and myself: Judi Bumstead, Carol Lacy, Pamela Johnson, Sandra Knowlton, Barbra Minar, Carolyn Johnson, Patti Cotter, and Beverley Hoogendyk.

Special thanks to Dr. Linda Christensen, Editorial Director, CompCare Publishers. I greatly cherish her support, caring, and belief in me.

I'd also like to express my gratitude to several seniors (aged seventy-six to ninety-six) who reside at the Solvang Lutheran Home in Solvang, California. They shared some of their vast wisdom on positive living with me: Grif, Peter, Sid, Maggie, Frieda, Oda, Ted, Marjorie, and Paul.

Thanks also to Clete, Phil, Dennis, Mark, David, Brad, and Rob for keeping Doug occupied on the tennis courts while I completed this project.

As always, my sincere appreciation to the physicians, therapists, pastors, teachers, and many others who told their stories and offered their insights so that this book would be possible.

May God bless and keep you all.

INTRODUCTION

Meghan listened to a woman on the "Oprah Winfrey Show" as she told the audience about growing up in a "dysfunctional" family and being "codependent" in her marriage. The woman described herself as an "adult child of divorce."

Meghan had heard these types of buzz words many times on both day-time talk shows and evening news-magazine programs. She'd read them in articles and books. Still, she didn't wholly understand how she could best use them to help make her own life more fulfilled.

Meghan is like many of us. Now, because of media influence, we have been torn apart, stripped down, and dissected into little, dysfunctional pieces, and we're not sure how to put ourselves together again. I believe the answer is to move on in order to live a life free of dysfunction.

If you are tired of the wear and tear of hearing all the bad news about people and our multitude of dysfunctions, you will be happy and relieved to see how you can take what you know, apply it to your life, and gain new insights to continue your healing, renew love in your relationships, and face the future with confidence and joy.

For decades, we've tried to escape the reality that whole and healthy lives often require tremendous effort to be created and sustained. Blinding ourselves to problems didn't work in the fifties. Free Love didn't work in the sixties. Divorce didn't work in the seventies. Money didn't work in the eighties. But reality *can* work in the nineties!

Reality means taking responsibility for our own life's fulfillment, regardless of our unique circumstances. We must accept that conflict, rejection, loss, grief, and hard decisions will be a part of life. But we can learn to cope, overcome, and find strength because we have survived even our deepest hurts.

Reality also means seeing our most significant relationships as circles of unending connections. We are, in fact, connected to our parents, siblings, spouses, and children forever, whether we like it or not.

The very essence of having a fulfilled and joyful life is being able to "circle" with others in healthy, loving relationships. This book begins with an exploration of the relationship you have with your self and then progresses to take you through an entire "circle process," showing you how to relate well to your partner, your children, and others. In each section you will find practical guidance to help you solve the problems that most of us experience as adults living in a very complex world.

From our earliest days, we have used circles in our lives. As children we played games with circles: "Musical Chairs" and "Ring Around the Rosy." We gave promise rings and I.D. bracelets to one another. We took pleasure in round foods: gumdrops, lollipops, and cookies.

We have circles as our symbols for male and female. The planet we live on is round; it rotates and moves around the sun. We identify with clichés, such as, "he ran around in circles. . . ." As adults we can use the circular concept as a way to understand and embrace our own process of moving on to come full circle and leave dysfunction behind. We want to be able to relax, love, play, and live with one another again—without fixating constantly on blame, shame, and dysfunction.

Maybe you've faced your personal problems, accepted that your growing up was less than perfect, and now you want to move on with your life. You may wonder if the pain, problems, or complications resulting from your past will ever stop. You may be an adult child of an alcoholic or a recovering addict. Or you may be the victim of your parents' divorce. You may have tried private therapy and support groups, or even educated yourself about the reality of reaching adulthood as a "broken" individual.

You've likely been honest with at least a few others about your own bad habits, codependencies, anxieties, shame, and relationship challenges. But lately you've noticed when you confide that you're an adult child, a recovering anorexic, or an obsessive-compulsive eater, others roll their eyes or become distant, as if to say, "When are you going to get through this?!"

You may have even wondered that yourself. But we do not live our lives alone or in a straight line, and we cannot simply erase our tragedies. We must be moving on to restore and renew our relationships. Coming full circle means integrating the reality of the past and present with healthy choices for future well-being. We all move this way to become whole, well-rounded people and to nurture all of who we truly are—without trying to cut and paste ourselves together from jagged, unrealistic pieces.

I know this to be true: true for myself and for more than 1,500 others whom I've contacted to write six books and create three videos. I know that it is also true for thousands more who've heard me on radio or television and responded.

This integration process has been the most exciting and healing adventure of my life. I am stronger, I love more intensely, and I enjoy life more fully. The good news is that you can too! Each case study is about real people (enough details have been changed to protect their privacy). Every exercise, quiz, and suggestion has been tried by people just like you and me—and found to be effective. I hope you will share in the excitement of the journey to gain knowledge, wisdom, and understanding so you, too, can begin a healthy life without dysfunction.

Part I

Self—The Inner Circle

This

Not this

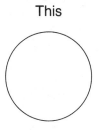

CHAPTER ONE
Finding Your Circle Shape

Betsy grew up in what she felt was a fairly normal, middle-class family. Sure, they had their problems but none remarkable enough to prompt Betsy to seek professional help. But she had a nagging feeling that pushed her to look more closely at her past and present life. She didn't always feel on top of the world.

Her marriage had its rocky peaks and valleys. She wasn't completely thrilled with her career, but she couldn't quite seem to make the necessary changes to advance. She had to admit that she felt some disappointment with motherhood. And she was constantly being called a dummy by her father, which did not help her self-esteem.

Hmmm. Maybe there was some value in delving into her past and examing her present more deeply. She sure hoped she wouldn't be stuck in the same place ten years from now. She wanted more fulfillment in her life. She wanted better relationships and more sincere love.

Betsy, along with many others, needs to consider how her past contributes to her present and how her present choices will contribute to her future happiness.

When we are healthy, we are like round circles in motion. But when we are functioning poorly, allowing shame, anger, and guilt to control us, we become oval, and we bump along in life much like an egg plunks around a table top. We can't get a rhythm of motion going strongly enough to operate smoothly. When we allow ourselves to live in misery and refuse to do something about it, we remain out of the circle shape and can't proceed beyond dysfunction.

I was on my own personal journey to come full circle when my friend Jackie found out that she had ovarian cancer. It immediately changed both our lives.

The months following the cancer diagnosis were filled with chaos and confusion. Jackie tried everything possible to help herself. She went to doctors, a therapist, an acupuncturist, and talked to a pastor. She read books on everything from conventional treatments to holistic healing. She went through several major surgeries and chemotherapy treatment. Nothing she tried slowed the progress of this wicked disease. It quickly spread to other organs and only a year after the initial diagnosis, Jackie's health had disintegrated and death was near. During this time we talked about everything—except her impending death. We could not voice what was on both our minds.

> One day during a visit to her, I burst into tears and blubbered without preface, "I don't want you to die!"

> Jackie looked at me with clear, calm eyes and whispered, "*I* don't want *me* to die."

The conversation that followed was emotional and probing. We talked about her life: what she regretted the most and what she enjoyed the most. We discussed our individual beliefs about God and the roles we thought God played in the scheme of things, even in her death; the death of a barely-forty-year-old wife and mother of three teenagers.

Jackie hated to think that she would not see her children marry or have the pleasure of being a grandmother. She asked me to watch out for her loved ones, who might blame God for her disease and possibly turn away, refusing to believe in God. She asked me to deliver a few personal messages for her when she was gone. Then she said something that I'd never really thought about before.

> "There is one thing I've had to learn on this journey toward death—how very true it is that we are born alone and we die

alone. The difference is what each of us does with our own life and how we will face God with what we did or did not do. No doctor, therapist, friend, family member, or acquaintance can stand in our place when it comes time to leave this world—we must each stand alone."

One day as I stood by Jackie's bed, I knew it was time to say good-bye. There were six others in the room. Jackie's eyes locked with mine. For a few fleeting seconds, it was as if no one else were there, and I saw the real person who had lived inside the frail body for so many months. I saw the "forever" woman who felt no pain and knew only joy and peace as she prepared to make her passage to Heaven.

As I leaned down to give her one last hug, Jackie pushed me away with the strength of a perfectly healthy person and said, "No! No hugs. No tears. Just, 'See ya later.'"

I swallowed hard, smiled widely, and nodded as I turned away. When I stopped at the doorway to look at her one last time, she threw me a kiss. And that was it.

As I walked down the hall, my tears of sorrow found their release. Jackie would meet God alone. As will I. As will you.

After Jackie's death, I began a new direction in my life—I kept a constant eye on being accountable for myself and the quality of my life. I realized for the first time what it meant to stand alone and take responsibility for myself, while living alongside others.

Years have passed. Jackie's children are full grown. Her daughter is married and has a baby. One son is also married and has his own business, while the other son is in college. Jackie's husband has since married a lovely woman, whose friendship I deeply value. Life has a funny way of pushing and pulling us along as it makes its own way ahead of us.

Our lives are like the childhood game, "The Farmer in the Dell." The farmer takes a wife; the wife takes a child; the child takes a dog; the dog takes a cat; the cat takes a mouse; the mouse takes the cheese; the cheese stands alone.

Most of us try at times to *take* people and activities into our lives so we can avoid our pains and sorrows. At times, it hurts to be solely accountable for ourselves. We often fear being completely alone. Yet we are separate, self-contained beings, and sometimes we must face a tragedy to help us fulfill our lives. We can surround ourselves with the best relationships—but only under the condition that our *own* lives fall into order as we go.

The first area of business, in terms of moving on to come full circle, is to stop, to mentally stand still, and to take stock of your own life. It is necessary—regardless of your past experiences in growing up, choosing a partner, having children, or choosing careers—to work toward a contented state of being. You do not need to carry a heavy burden of shame, nor do you need to blame others for your disappointments and unhappiness.

No Shame, No Blame

You may already have heard how shame can affect your life negatively. Shame, along with anger, guilt, and codependency, are all issues that became prominent in the 1980s.

Shame can be an incredibly powerful, vaporous emotion that painfully controls our reactions to life.

Allison is a good example of how insidiously shame can eat away at personal happiness and be a divisive force in relationships. Allison is thirty-seven years old. She grew up in a middle-class family, the third of four children. Her father was a white-collar professional and her mother a homemaker.

Allison's childhood appeared to be perfect. There was no overt abuse related to alcohol or other drugs, physical violence, or sexual molestation.

Allison didn't lack for material goods. She wore nice clothes, had her own bedroom, and fit in well with the popular girls her age. She arrived at school each morning feeling well-fed, groomed, and prepared.

Early in my discussions with Allison, I began to hear things that set off tiny alarms: something had affected her life so strongly that she felt herself to be completely inadequate. I kept a file of her comments until they added up to an identifiable issue: shame.

Allison's childhood was peppered with memories of being ridiculed, criticized, and shamed. She recalled that family members teased one another mercilessly for any little mistake or fault. She clearly remembered overhearing her parents discuss the problems of others in judgmental and shaming tones:

> "Isn't it awful about that Stewart boy? His poor parents must be so ashamed!"

> "What a pity that the Morgans can't control their own children!"

> "Did you hear about that ungrateful Oliver girl? She went and got herself pregnant!"

> "I feel so sorry for that fat Johnson child. She eats like a pig. Her parents must be so embarrassed!"

The messages to Allison were constant and clear: what you *do* is who you *are*, and if you don't do the "right" things you risk being shamed—deeply shamed.

Allison's adolescence was riddled with shaming directives:

> "Wash your face or you'll never get rid of those pimples!"

> "Are those stretch marks on your legs?! Good grief! You'd better get yourself on a diet."

> "Wipe that makeup off your face, you look like a hooker!"

> "Why would you want to date *that* goofball? We raised you to have better taste than that!"

The shameful messages intensified Allison's feelings that what she did was enmeshed with who she was—and that who she was never quite measured up. Her parents laughed when she said she wanted to be a geologist; they wanted her to be a teacher or a nurse.

As a young adult, Allison scrambled to be good enough. She wasn't conscious of any of this as it happened to her, of course, but children learn what they live and become programmed to operate on automatic pilot.

In college, Allison cringed at any grade lower than a "B." She felt queasy if the scale climbed three pounds higher than the month before. As a working woman, she hung her head when her boss reminded her of a procedure she'd overlooked.

As a new bride, Allison was particularly anxious to please. When her husband merely asked her why she chose to wear a certain outfit, she changed clothes, assuming that her first choice wasn't appropriate.

As a mother, Allison was exemplary. Her children were groomed, well-fed, dressed nicely, and prepared when they went to school—just as Allison had been as a child.

For years Allison's life was directed by an inner core of shame. It constantly reminded her that what she did was who she was. And who she was did not satisfy the intense standards the shame demanded.

Allison's adult life was dysfunctional—not working well and unnecessarily painful—in almost every area because she spent so much time trying to live up to the unrealistic expectations and rules she had learned in childhood. As an adult, Allison perpetuated the shame messages from her past and unwittingly carried them out in her marriage and in her parenting.

When Allison's children were teenagers, the frantic pace of always trying to be good enough caught up with her. Her shame bubbled up and blistered on the surface of her life. She collapsed emotionally, crumbling under the sheer weight of trying to accomplish the impossible: perfection.

Her daughter was dating a juvenile delinquent. Her son was flunking junior high. Her husband was distant. Allison was positive that it was her fault, that *she* was defective. But she was also full of rage because her loved ones refused to measure up to *her* standards—just as she and her siblings had refused to measure up to their own parents' impossibly high standards.

After Allison's collapse, she went into therapy and discovered that shame was at the core of her behavior. She realized that she had learned to suppress her natural instincts and to respond to life through the examples set by her parents. Allison faced the fact that her shame-filled childhood caused her to be uncomfortable inside her own skin; she was ashamed of who she was.

In *Healing the Shame That Binds You,* John Bradshaw writes, "When our instinctual life is shamed, the natural core of our life is bound up. It's like an acorn going through excruciating agony for becoming an oak, or a flower feeling ashamed for blossoming."

Allison proceeded to explore how her family of origin had caused her pain and how her past affected her present. In order to get beyond those issues, however, Allison had to accept the fact that she was solely responsible for her own well-being. She had to work through her feelings of shame on her own. She could hold her parents accountable for her problems, but that would not solve anything. Allison had to learn a most freeing lesson: not to *blame* others for her unhappiness.

Blame only perpetuates shame. Most of our parents did the absolute best they could to raise us. We must learn to accept others and ourselves at the levels of capability they, and we, happen to be. We are each in a different "place" in life on any given day.

Yes, of course, we can understand why adult children of alcoholics, victims of sexual abuse, or physically battered individuals have problems. We can look into our backgrounds and see that the roots of our challenges often come from what we learned growing up. Our parents very likely acted out the programming of their parents, and so on—for many generations and in a variety of ways.

In therapy, Allison resisted this philosophy at first. She wanted to blame all of her pain on her parents. It was their fault she was so deeply ashamed; therefore, if she cut them out of her life, she would be okay.

Wrong. Just as a severely abused child will often choose to live with the abusive parents rather than with foster parents in a safe and protected environment, an adult like Allison can't completely deny herself the love and attachment she has for her family of origin, at least not for very long.

It would be better for Allison to use her background as a tool for gaining knowledge, wisdom, and understanding. She should use what she learns to become better and stronger, but not to try to obliterate the relationships that are vital to her identity.

Don't misunderstand me. I'm not saying that abuse in any form is acceptable or that we should embrace our extended families and love them at the expense of our own health or happiness. I am saying that for the *sake* of our health and happiness, we should learn not to *blame* them for our present misery.

For example, Allison needed only minimal contact with her parents in order for her to sort through her own problems and feelings. Finally, she could fully accept herself as she was and love her parents as they were. She never completely cut ties with them. To do so might bring more pain and heartache upon herself than she could bear. She merely needed some distance to make her own choices—to reshape herself from a bumping oval into a rolling circle. One of the things Allison discovered was this well-known saying: Hindsight is NOT always 20-20!

Do you have a memory of a place you used to know during your childhood? Have you visited that place as an adult, only to realize how much smaller it is than you remembered? Emotional memories that linger and threaten your stability may also be reduced in size when you look at them realistically as an adult.

In Allison's case, she found several things she could eliminate from her belief system. For instance, she absorbed a message from her parents that echoed in her subconscious, "Fat people are worthless."

As an adult, Allison constantly fought to lose ten or fifteen pounds to reduce herself to what she considered her ideal size. This struggle didn't originate from a sound mind. For Allison's height and bone structure, she fell almost exactly in the middle of the acceptable weight category on her doctor's chart.

However, as she delved into why this was such an issue for her, she realized that her mother had a habit of pointing out others whom she deemed "fat." Allison listened to this for years and unwittingly picked up a message that it was shameful to be overweight.

This was not something that her mother did *to* Allison. It was something Allison interpreted on her own. As an adult, Allison had to remember her mother's habit and recall her own reaction. What she found was pleasantly surprising to her. First, she realized that her mother's reaction to overweight people was most likely a knee-jerk response to her own insecurities. Probably *not* coincidentally, Allison's mother was usually ten or fifteen pounds overweight and struggled to shed those unwanted pounds just as Allison did.

By constantly comparing herself with people who were often more overweight than she was and passing judgment on them, Allison's mother was able to feel better about her own weight.

When Allison realized that there was no personal bias toward *her* in her mother's criticism of overweight people, she could look more objectively at her own struggle with weight. She realized that as a child she took on her mother's definition of what a "right" size should be. Now Allison could clear her hindsight, step back, and determine as an adult what she wanted her weight to be. Much to her delight, Allison found that she needn't struggle anymore! She was a healthy weight for her unique body frame. She felt good physically, and emotionally she only needed to untie the invisible cords that connected her to her mother.

In my own adult life, I moved beyond dysfunction about monetary issues by realizing that I had absorbed a very unrealistic view of people and their financial status while growing up.

Until I was ten years old, I lived in a modest home on several acres outside of town. My memories are of being free, playing outdoors, and feeling completely secure. Then my parents built a beautiful new home with brand new furniture. We also had a swimming pool, a boat, three snowmobiles, and two new cars. Over the next few years, my previously quiet, gently rolling life seemed to explode.

Overnight I felt the self-contained family I'd known since birth being pulled into a faster lane. People started coming over for social gatherings because my parents had the biggest house, a pool, and plenty of grown-up toys. Friends from my new school wanted to come to my house; they said their homes were boring.

Suddenly our family was in the limelight. Everyone knew who I was, and I subconsciously took on unfortunate attitudes about money: People only liked you for what you had, and you were only as good as your material worth.

This was not something my parents taught me intentionally. They were not the least bit interested in climbing the social ladder. However, as a young child I interpreted an abundance of money to mean an abundance of friends and increased social status.

When I became a wife and mother struggling with finances (as most young homemakers do), shame's ugly presence stared me in the eye. I was reluctant to entertain guests in my home, and I avoided getting close to people I felt had greater wealth or status than I had. I felt ashamed that I couldn't afford a big, fancy house, hired help, or expensive summer camps for my kids. Emotionally, I hid in my shame and very likely missed many opportunities to meet some wonderful people.

As I entered my thirties, it began to dawn on me that my hindsight of childhood beliefs about material wealth was anything but 20-20! My parents had worked hard for their money. They just happened to begin to enjoy it at a time when I was very impressionable. I began to clear my vision by taking a careful look around me as well as looking inside myself.

I defined my needs, wants, and goals. I stopped comparing myself to others. I struck up new friendships with people from all walks of life and forced myself beyond the anxiety that came from shame. Today my life is filled with people from all income levels. I no longer question my self-worth, because my worth comes from being human, not from material possessions.

It is essential that we establish a habit of examining our pasts when issues become painful in the present. However, it is just as essential that we take responsibility for solving our own problems and not try to blame them on others. No shame, no blame. That's a big step toward coming full circle.

Contending for Your Niche

Most people have a profound need to find their own particular niche in life. Whether it is a teacher who dreams of being a country music star, a corporate executive who wants to make a living on the professional golf tour, or a secretary who fantasizes about building a cabin in the mountains, people spend their lives longing to find a special niche in the world—that's customized for their personality.

People often expend a lot of energy in dreaming. That's fine, as long as dreaming is not a way of avoiding responsibility for themselves or for their personal happiness.

A man I know says he can't afford to try his hand at a career in forestry because he lives in the desert and has family obligations. He has the same hectic, twenty-four-hour days as his neighbor, yet his neighbor is fulfilling his dream of running a recreational tour business by working nights. He takes tourists into the desert in his four-wheel-drive jeep after he finishes with a full day on the job. He drives for an hour and is home by 7:00 P.M. to spend quality time with his family.

We all have twenty-four hours in each day. The difference is how we spend our twenty-four hours and whether we choose to commit to finding our personal niche. It does no good to blame anyone else for our lack of ambition, desire, or financial means, because there isn't anyone else responsible for our disappointments.

We must be working on fulfilling our own lives and creatively making them significant in *our eyes* as we learn to relate better with others.

Catherine Bateson, author of *Composing a Life*, has been quoted as saying:

> "We are all engaged in a day-to-day process of self-invention—not discovery. What we search for does not exist until we find it. Both the past and the future are raw material, shaped and re-shaped by each individual."

I was very fortunate. Even as a child, I knew that I wanted to be a writer. I began in a very plain, unglamorous way—I wrote letters to my relatives. As a young teenager in love for the first time, I wrote poems.

And shortly thereafter I began keeping journals and notes of all kinds. I now have a collection of writings that are more than twenty years old, which chronicles the growth from young girl into adult woman, wife, and mother.

This was not a conscious decision. It was something I was driven naturally to do. I didn't question it at fifteen, but there have been many moments of doubt since then. When I sat up all night writing at my kitchen table and cared for two small children during the day, I seriously questioned my common sense. I poured over lessons from my correspondence courses in writing while my friends shopped.

I wondered what was wrong with me. When other couples began surpassing us financially because I chose to be a stay-at-home mom—who developed creative ideas and wrote literature, instead of getting a savvy white-collar job—I prayed to be transformed magically into a "normal" person.

But over the years, I've come to appreciate my drive and the eccentricities that help define who I am. I have chosen to fit into a personal niche in life that doesn't mean I will always be financially stable. It sometimes isn't very convenient for my husband or children, and I'm not always able to accommodate my friends or extended family members. But the price is worth it, and I take full responsibility for the choice I have made.

It wasn't always like this, however. During tough times, I tended to blame anyone or anything (but myself) for negative consequences. It was the economy. My husband wasn't giving me enough emotional support. My kids needed too much of my time. I didn't have a nice enough office, a computer system, or the appropriate education. The bills weighed too heavily on my mind, and the phone rang too often. I just couldn't concentrate on my work.

As I progressed, I saw how vital it was to refuse to give in to the stumbling blocks I encountered. I learned I had to make the choices necessary to contend for my separate niche—and commit to sticking with those choices.

If our inner circles are going to be shaped for smooth motion and not squelched into the egg shapes of dysfunction, we have to be prepared to make choices that don't always feel right. We have to know that because most of us are dysfunctional adults to one degree or another, our feelings don't always agree with what is best for us.

We may sometimes have to learn to trust our heads as well as our hearts. One thing is certain: choices based solely on our intellectual knowledge *or* our emotional feelings will *always* bring some sort of consequence to ourselves and others. We must use both head and heart to consider every choice carefully: are we willing to pay the consequences that will follow?

Make Your Choices Count!

We have all made choices we later regret. Even if it's insignificant, like choosing the wrong color shirt, we may be reminded of our error by co-workers who cannot let us forget the fact that the lavender shirt doesn't match the peach paisley skirt. Finally, we are motivated to throw the shirt away, donate it to charity, or take it to a consignment store. Then the mistake is hidden, and we hope we have gained better judgment from our embarrassing experience.

Some choices have much more severe consequences. A young teen gets pregnant. Her inner circle may be oval shaped for years as she adjusts to growing up overnight and being forced to care for another human being's welfare. A man gets drunk one night and ends up in bed with a woman other than his wife. He wrestles with the consequences of his choice for a long time. Should he tell his wife? Will he get caught? What if his wife leaves him? What will happen to their relationship?

An entrepreneur sinks his wife's inheritance into *his* lifelong dream. He loses every penny. Now he, she, and their children have to live with the consequences of *his* choices.

If we are going to have whole inner circles and leave dysfunction behind, we must learn to make our choices carefully and be ready to pay the price necessary to follow through. You may get a resounding, "Yes!" from your family when you tell them you've decided to open up a retail store. But believe me, when you're gone from home sixty hours a week, struggling to keep the business afloat, you will be the "cheese that stands alone" when they express their disapproval and wrath.

We make many choices individually that change the course of our personal lives. So it is important that we make each choice count, if only in our own minds.

Michelle will turn forty this year. She has gone through several emotionally straining months. Her life just isn't what she envisioned it to be. When she graduated from college with a liberal arts degree, she assumed that she would get a job, get married, have a couple of kids, and settle into a fairly comfortable lifestyle.

In the beginning, her plan unfolded without disappointments or surprises. She landed a job as an assistant to a hospital administrator. Within a year she was engaged to marry a young doctor. Two years later she was pregnant with their first child. She then decided to quit her job and stay home to raise the baby. Three years later she had a second child. However, by her thirtieth birthday, Michelle had encountered several disappointments. She then began to doubt the wisdom of her choices.

First, she'd discovered that being a doctor's wife had some distinct drawbacks: her husband necessarily put a great deal of energy into his profession; he was on call most of the time and didn't have much of himself left over for Michelle.

Second, she was pressured by the community to give more of her "free" time. Board members asked her to do volunteer projects, make appearances at fund-raising events, and to participate in cliquish social activities that she didn't care for.

Third, she had two young children to raise, which wasn't quite as easy as she had anticipated. Michelle was tired, lonesome for her husband, and hungry for the compassion she knew he showered on his patients.

When both kids were in school, Michelle decided to go back to work. However, she found that she lacked the skills and training necessary to get a fulfilling job. In place of a job, she took a variety of adult education classes that only satisfied her personal curiosities. As her fortieth birthday approached, Michelle felt empty, discouraged, and cheated out of the life she thought she deserved.

"When I was twenty, I thought the world was an open book for me to enjoy. When I was thirty, I assumed I was just barely into the heart of the book. Now I feel like my life is half over—the book is half read—and I'm not that excited about continuing to turn the pages," Michelle said.

"There's this pall that hangs over some of the choices I've made. I don't think I would marry a doctor again. I need to be the major focus of my partner's life. My husband has to be married to his profession first, and me second. This situation has forced me to raise our kids largely on my own. I'm the one who tucks them in, says prayers with them, goes to all their school functions, and deals with the angst of adolescence.

"I think I would also choose a specific profession. I'm not really trained for anything. I feel like I'm in limbo, and the choices I make from here on out better count for something. I feel like I'm running out of time. I don't even have meaningful friendships because I've spent so much of my life waiting for things to change.

"My husband networks with all kinds of people. My kids have their friends and separate interests. All I have is a few courses in cake decorating and art expression under my belt. I feel totally let down by life."

Michelle seems to want to blame others for her disappointment. She appears to justify her unhappiness by blaming it on the kind of man she married and by martyring herself to raise the children.

Michelle made choices she thought would contribute to her fulfillment; but she didn't make them count. She passively waited for her relationships to somehow, magically fill her up. We simply can't do this if we are to be happy. We must dig in, take responsibility for our choices, and move on with a distinct course of action.

There will be times as we grow and change when we fall back into our old behavior habits: justification, shame, blame, and negative reactions. But we can learn to recognize these and alter them before we are pulled down into hopeless despair. We must choose to control how we respond to life and not give away our personal power. When we leave behind old patterns of behavior that keep us like ovals instead of like circles, we can make new commitments to achieve personal fulfillment and happiness.

When Old Patterns Haunt You

I can't count the number of times I've convinced myself that I've overcome ineffective habits only to find myself later relying on them when the pressure's on. For instance, I know that I shouldn't rescue my children from the consequences of their choices, so I have intentionally allowed them to fend for themselves. Yet, when they get into trouble, my immediate reaction is still to get them out of the mess. I should stick to my beliefs, keep my distance, evaluate the situation objectively, and then decide whether or not to intervene. If I interfere, I will only be teaching them to rely on me or others for happiness and to blame others for their misery.

I do the same thing with my husband. I often want to jump in and fix things for him, too—often with resentful self-righteousness. And then I wonder why he won't do things for himself. Why would he? If someone always cleaned my bathrooms for me, I surely wouldn't clean them myself!

Over the years, I have learned to recognize when I've fallen into patterns of focusing on others, which sacrifices my well-being and causes me to plunk along as an oval rather than rolling smoothly as a round circle. When these old patterns return to haunt me, I follow three steps.

    1. STOP
    2. EXAMINE
    3. ALTER THE COURSE

For instance, I am extremely sensitive to my environment and tend to get anxious very easily. When I notice physical symptoms of anxiety—

pounding heart, shortness of breath, or stomach cramps—I mentally STOP myself. I then EXAMINE the circumstances and question *why* I feel so anxious. If I feel anxious before a radio interview, for example, I may realize that I'm nervous about my performance. Then I ALTER THE COURSE by deliberately thinking or doing something other than what I was thinking or doing *before* my symptoms appeared. I may jog in place a few minutes or repeat a short phrase in my head such as, "I am calm and relaxed. I am calm and relaxed."

This sounds very simple, and it usually works. Sometimes I don't even need to worry about using my techniques. I can often go right to the interview and have other things on my mind. More often than not, I am so distracted, I forget about being anxious. But, if this doesn't happen and if my three-step process fails me, it's still okay. I'm not perfect. I have limitations and weaknesses just like everyone else. This is something we often forget when we feel we've failed.

So when old patterns haunt me, I do the best I can and take it from there. I use it as a learning tool. Maybe I'll do something different before the next interview. I may choose to prepare more thoroughly—or more likely not prepare as much. Or I may put more thought into scheduling the interview (mornings are awful for me). Regardless of what I may do, I stop myself, examine my situation, and take absolute responsibility to alter the course in whatever way I can.

You can do it too. If you find your job or home life depressing, you can STOP. You can EXAMINE why you are depressed. And you can choose to ALTER THE COURSE by doing some things differently. If your depression continues to deepen, you can change a few more things. Of course, if these steps don't work, it may be an important signal to see a doctor or other professional.

These are the first steps to leaving dysfunction behind and becoming a whole circle within yourself:

1. Accept that you stand alone in taking responsibility for your own happiness.

2. Start fresh by exploring the ways shame is controlling your life and resolve to stop blaming people or things for *your* unhappiness.

3. Realize that hindsight is NOT always 20-20 and that you may be allowing certain beliefs—now obsolete—to haunt your life.

4. Vow to yourself that it's worth the struggle to contend for your very own niche in life.

5. Make your choices count and be prepared to take sole responsibility for paying the consequences or accepting the rewards.

6. Know that when old, ineffective patterns of behavior haunt you, you are in control and can STOP, EXAMINE, and ALTER THE COURSE.

Reflect on how your childhood and adult past may now be negatively influencing you. Look for possible areas of shame, blame, and inaccurate hindsight. Notice where you gave up your dreams because you feared not finding your niche. Examine the times in your life when you made the wrong choices. Learn from these mistakes.

Pay close attention to the areas where old behaviors and feelings haunt your present life. These are clues to the roots of a multitude of problems in our lives. Try the following exercise to see if you have experienced any situations that may have caused you to be an oval egg.

Exercise: Looking for Eggs

If there are areas of your life that are keeping you plunking along instead
of rolling smoothly, you may find that completing the following chart
will help you. Nearly all painful issues can be traced to circumstances or
choices in our past. Whether it's a childhood experience from your family of origin, a time when a lover humiliated you in front of others, or
the fact that you spent nonexistent money on new golf clubs, I think
you'll find this charting exercise useful. Use Allison's messages about
weight and Michelle's early choices as examples:

Year	Memory or Incident	Predominant Feelings Then

Symptoms in Your Life Now	What You Can Do to Alter the Course

CHAPTER TWO

"Emotional Insecurities Account"

This entire chapter is devoted to explaining how our insecurities contribute to keeping us out of circle shape. They are, very often, at the root of *why* we do the things we do. My theory is that we all have an "emotional insecurities account." We make deposits—one little or large hurt at a time—like money to a savings account. We also make deposits when we compare ourselves unfavorably to others, when we worry about nonsensical things, or when we are afraid for no particular reason. Then, when the account gets to a certain balance, it starts accumulating interest in the form of anger, jealousy, criticism, ridicule, and other negative attitudes.

We are all insecure about some things. And as we establish intimate relationships, those close to us are bound to stumble onto our insecurities. Likewise, we notice others' insecurities by their negative reactions. This is powerful insight; we may abuse this knowledge by getting others to do what we want or to see things our way. If we know which buttons to push on others' "automatic teller machines," we can make withdrawals from their emotional insecurities account for our own benefit.

I've found that the only sure way to get rid of each of these "accounts" is to examine the record books and to voluntarily close the accounts. Just as we have learned it is important to be responsible for our own choices, we also have to be responsible for our own emotional insecurities accounts. If we don't, we remain oval, rocking to and fro, and do not enjoy the full life of a smoothly rolling circle.

Brenda knows all about these accounts. She and her husband, Jeff, were recently forced to examine some of their insecurities:

> Brenda and Jeff were getting ready to go out to dinner with friends. Brenda emerged from the bathroom and asked Jeff eagerly, "How do I look?"
>
> Jeff glanced over and said, "Fine. But I thought you said you were going to wear your green dress."
>
> Brenda's face fell. She spoke a little more crisply than she meant to, "Why?! Don't you like the red one?"
>
> Impatient, Jeff rolled his eyes. "I didn't even say anything close to that. I just thought you said you were going to wear the green dress."
>
> Brenda snapped, "I think the red one looks better!"

Jeff sighed and turned back to his closet to get a shirt. He knew that Brenda would be cold and snippy all night. She was like that—one little thing would set her off and she would be defensive for hours. She was so insecure! He didn't understand it! He could say something completely innocent and straightforward, and she would interpret it as an insult.

Sure enough. Brenda was curt and ill-tempered during their entire dinner. During dessert, the conversation with their friends turned to calorie-counting. Jeff remarked that Brenda was always watching her figure. He meant exactly what he said. And what he said was true.

> Brenda, however, quickly read a deeper meaning into the comment. She hissed, "Are you saying I'm fat?"

Jeff stared at her open-mouthed. How could such a simple statement cause so much resentment? As Jeff recovered from Brenda's sting, she hurled a personal jab at him.

> "You're someone to talk anyway! You've been twenty pounds overweight since we got back from our honeymoon!"

That did it! Brenda knew how sensitive he was about his weight! How could she be so spiteful?

> Jeff narrowed his eyes and said in a deceptively humorous tone, "Brenda hit that nail square on the head. I did put on the pounds right after we were married—because her cooking is so full of fats and starches!"

As Jeff and Brenda locked eyes, the other couple shifted their chairs away from the table uncomfortably and suggested that they all leave.

As the four of them exited the restaurant, Brenda wondered about her marriage. Things were worse than they had ever been between her and Jeff. They used to be able to spend a casual night out without bickering. Now it seemed they couldn't even get through a meal without attacking each other!

A few days later, Brenda decided to examine the way she interacted with Jeff, to find out why they always ended up hostile and cold. She remembered the incident about the dresses first. Why had she assumed the worst when Jeff only asked her a question about her clothing? It wasn't as if he'd criticized her.

Brenda felt disgusted with herself. She was so insecure! But why? If she understood why she was sensitive to Jeff's question, maybe she could start to unravel some of her problems.

Brenda thought about her sensitivity. She'd always worried about whether she looked attractive. Why? That was *easy* to answer. She'd grown up watching her father pass judgment on her mother's appearance and compare his wife unfavorably with other women.

In fact, Brenda's father had complained incessantly that her mother had no taste in clothes, accessories, makeup, or hair styles. When Brenda remembered her mother, she thought of a frightened little rabbit, scurrying around to escape a predator. Brenda had vowed as a teenager never to let any man run her down like her father did to her mother.

Insecure? Of course, Brenda was insecure about her appearance. But it had nothing at all to do with Jeff. Brenda had deposited her pain from childhood into her own emotional insecurities account without even knowing it.

When Brenda and Jeff got married, neither of them was aware that this particular account was full of insecurity. Each time Jeff made a comment or asked a question about her appearance, Brenda unwittingly made a deposit.

When the account was filled to capacity, Brenda could no longer contain her hurt. Her account began paying interest in the form of retaliatory anger, sarcasm, vengeful remarks, and wrongful blame.

Brenda shared her thoughts with Jeff. He immediately identified with her theory because he thought her father was a callous, inconsiderate, male chauvinist. Jeff reassured Brenda that she was beautiful and that he would be sensitive to her insecurity about her appearance.

Jeff also told her she had stumbled onto a great way for each of them to examine their insecurities. They agreed that they should try to understand each other's feelings and work them out together.

We all have accounts like Brenda's in which our hurts, fears, frustrations, irritations, and disappointments are deposited. The only way to rid ourselves of these accounts, or make them more manageable, is to make withdrawals and empty them. It would not have done any good for Brenda to blame her father and Jeff for her negative feelings. She needed to see that it was *she* alone who chose how to react to their comments about her appearance.

Look into your own life and find areas to which you react strongly or are particularly emotional; these are the clues to your deepest insecurities. There you will find your emotional insecurities account. You've probably been making deposits to your account for a long time. You've probably reaped interest payments in the form of negative reactions to non-threatening situations. And you may find that you've pushed the buttons of others' "automatic teller machines" when it was to your benefit to get a rise out of them. Step by step, one at a time, you *can* make withdrawals and empty your own account!

Making Deposits

What areas of your life consistently give you trouble? Finances? Career struggles? Marital strife? Parenting frustrations? Think about it. List the separate issues along one side of a piece of paper. Don't try to solve every problem you've ever had at one sitting. Simply list the two or three most prominent burdens you have right now—or the ones that have given you trouble since childhood.

For example, two concerns had haunted Zoe for years and another had appeared more recently:

○ She did not have a college degree.

○ She had stretch marks on her stomach.

○ Her eldest child left home.

These are three of Zoe's deposits in her emotional insecurities account. Zoe had her first child when she was seventeen. At the time, college seemed out of the question. As Zoe grew older, she felt even more insecure about not having a degree. She compared herself to others and found herself on the wanting end. She was oversensitive when people asked her about her educational background. She defended and justified herself endlessly.

Zoe made deposits to this account by being oversensitive and defensive when anyone commented on her lack of education—even if the person was merely complimenting her on her talents and accomplishments.

She also felt self-conscious about the stretch marks on her stomach. While her friends paraded around the municipal pool—feeling good about their bodies—she kept hers out of sight. As a teenager, she was devastated by such comparisons!

Each time Zoe looked at photographs of models in a fashion magazine, shopped for a swimsuit, or looked in a mirror, she made another deposit to her account. She convinced herself that she was grotesquely scarred for life.

Recently, Zoe experienced her third trauma when her son left home. She practically drove herself crazy mulling over dozens of questions. Was she a good parent? Did she and her husband set good examples for him? Had they loved him enough? Given him enough? Disciplined him too much? Would he know how to take care of himself? Did they instill sound moral values? Would he be responsible in his decisions about alcohol and other drugs, sex, and money?

Zoe continued to torture herself until she was an emotional wreck. She deposited so much to her account in so little time that it was full in a matter of days!

These are examples of accounts and deposits. Beside each concern you listed for yourself, write down the ways that *you* make deposits to your account. Now let's look at how interest payments are made.

Interest Payments

The insecurity Zoe felt about not having a college degree paid interest in two forms:

○ She held herself back in her career. She did not aggressively pursue some avenues and completely avoided others because she feared ridicule. Even though she used her public relations skills to the point of exhaustion and her business was highly profitable, Zoe still felt inadequate.

○ She also avoided intellectual conversations with peers because she feared they would view her as inferior to them.

Interest payments regarding her stretch marks were mainly avoidance tactics:

○ Zoe didn't go to pools or beaches for a long time. She was afraid someone might dare ask her why she was wearing a one-piece suit instead of a bikini! Her embarrassment about her body complicated her life.

○ Zoe was jealous of girls with smooth, tanned stomachs. Without even realizing why, she kept her distance from them. She now knows that she was afraid of her husband comparing them to her and seeing her as fat. For years, Zoe's husband never knew about her insecurity—he only wondered why a woman who once loved the water now resisted swimming, water-skiing, and sunbathing.

In fact, when he pushed Zoe to participate in these activities, she would get irritable and eventually angry, which resulted in more interest payments.

Interest payments stemming from Zoe's eldest child leaving home were immediate and turbulent:

> ○ She was depressed and cried a lot.
>
> ○ She acted hostile toward her husband and younger son.
>
> ○ She became anxious and worried.
>
> ○ She ran up a huge phone bill.

On your own list, note the various interest payments you experience from your insecurities. Do you get grouchy over trivial things? Are you afraid to try new things? Do you have phobias or other reactions that hold you back?

Eventually, Zoe wised up and looked realistically at her emotional insecurities account. She decided that she'd been oval long enough and wanted out of the destructive restrictions she had imposed on herself—she wanted to be a round circle again! She began to make withdrawals from her account.

Making Withdrawals

When Zoe got tired of reaping unwanted interest payments, she examined her record and devised ways to make withdrawals:

1. She carefully implemented a plan to complete her college degree. Meanwhile, she worked on improving her self-esteem and confidence. She also realized that life experience often educates people

much more thoroughly than academic learning; she need not be ashamed or insecure. Anyone who rejected her because she didn't have a degree was not worth working for. She chose to complete her college education for her personal satisfaction—not for anyone else's!

2. Zoe pondered about just how much the stretch marks on her stomach *really* bothered her. Enough to spend thousands of dollars for a tummy tuck? Nah. She asked herself, "If they don't bother me that much, then what's the big deal?" The answer was, "It wasn't." What was she continuously agonizing over? She was normal, just like everyone else. She began to see that most women were built like her—with curves and fleshy skin—not anorexically boney like the model she had tried to become. That realization was all it took for Zoe to recognize her distorted view of her physical appearance.

   Zoe is now much more comfortable with her body. She doesn't compare herself to other women. Her self-esteem has grown immensely since she started appreciating her physical attributes. When she was secure enough to share her former fears with her husband, he was shocked. He had hardly noticed her stretch marks.

3. Zoe talked herself out of her worries about her son leaving home: for every worry and concern she had, she made an objective counterattack.

   "Can he take care of himself?" was responded with, "Of course he can—you've taught him everything from how to clean a bathroom to how to balance his checkbook!" "Will he make responsible decisions regarding alcohol and other drugs, sex, and money?" was met with "Maybe not, but that's his choice—not mine! And I know he can deal with the consequences."

This is an important thing to remember: only try to make changes you have control over! Only you can make withdrawals from your emotional insecurities account. Your choices belong to you. You choose how to look at your insecurities, as well as other related problems, and you choose how to cope with them. Nobody else can do this for you. You may feel insecure about things that don't bother others and vice versa. Withdrawals involve taking the deposits "out" where you can examine them honestly and objectively. Only then can you consciously decide what to do about each issue. On your list, write down several different ways you can change your attitudes about your insecurities. For example, you may be insecure about asking for a promotion at work. You've unknowingly made these deposits:

○ You listened to others tell you horror stories about the boss.
○ You criticized yourself for your shortcomings.
○ You doubted your ability to handle a more responsible position.

Your account has destructively paid interest:

○ You put off asking for the promotion.
○ You feel anxious about your application.
○ You are irritable with family members.

You can make withdrawals by looking at your situation and carefully choosing realistic ways to handle the issue. You could . . .

○ Forget about asking for a promotion.
○ Take classes that relate to your prospective promotion.
○ Ask for the promotion and see what happens.

Regardless of what you choose to do, you are making withdrawals from your emotional insecurities account and increasing your self-esteem. The next step is to close your account.

Closing Your Account

Closing an emotional insecurities account is a five-step process. You've already begun most of the steps:

1. LIST EACH INSECURITY THAT CURRENTLY PLAGUES YOU.

2. TAKE INVENTORY OF YOUR NEGATIVE FEELINGS, THE DEPOSITS YOU MAKE. HOW DO YOU ALLOW THEM TO EXIST?

3. EXAMINE HOW EACH INSECURITY EXPRESSES ITSELF OR MAKES AN
    INTEREST PAYMENT IN YOUR LIFE.

4. BRAINSTORM FOR WAYS YOU CAN RESOLVE YOUR INSECURITIES
    OR MAKE WITHDRAWALS.

5. PREPARE YOURSELF TO DEAL WITH FUTURE INSECURITIES AND
    CLOSE THE ACCOUNT.

Very few problems that have recurred in our lives are gone for good. Like arthritis, they tend to return during the damp, cloudy days to hinder us and give us pain. The answer is to be prepared!

Michael was very insecure about how he measured up to his father-in-law, Mr. Burdock, who was a highly successful and domineering businessman. Michael was a soft-spoken, less ambitious man. His emotional insecurities account haunted him for ten years before he finally dealt with it. He looked at the deposits made to his account:

1. Michael grew up in poverty and absorbed the belief that everyone should want to be financially successful.

2. Michael had a teacher in high school who teased him for not being athletic; some of his peers used to call him "fag" because of his slight build.

3. Michael's wife worshiped her father and constantly compared Michael to him.

After reviewing his deposits, Michael discovered why he was insecure and how he allowed his negative feelings to exist. He look at the interest payments:

○ He felt guilty for not being ambitious.
○ He feared rejection and ridicule.
○ He covered up his insecurities with defensiveness.
○ He was contentious with his father-in-law; he was endlessly defending his job, his family, and his ambitions.

Michael easily saw how he reacted to his insecurities. This insight enabled him to design ways to make withdrawals. He made a list of three men he knew who had small builds, were content with their lives, and who were well-respected. He folded this list and put it in his wallet. When he began to feel insecure in his father-in law's presence, Michael mentally scanned the list to remind himself that those he had listed were content and respected people and that he could be, too.

He then wrote a short list of affirmations and repeated them silently to himself in the shower each morning:

> "I am a lovable, worthwhile human being. I am successful in my own life. I am accountable only for my own happiness."

Michael explained his feelings to his wife. This took a lot of courage; his fear of rejection and ridicule had previously prevented him from sharing his feelings with her. To his astonishment, his wife was extremely compassionate and understanding. She told Michael that she'd had no idea that she was comparing him to her father. She assured Michael that if money and ambition were more important to her than kindness and honesty, she would have married someone like her father. She also promised to be sensitive and to assert herself in Michael's favor.

These withdrawals helped Michael so much that he became more at ease around Mr. Burdock and less contentious. He closed his account by preparing himself to feel insecure again:

1. He thought of several topics he was knowledgeable about that he could discuss with Mr. Burdock. This relaxed Michael and gave him confidence before an encounter with his father-in-law.

2. Michael vowed that if Mr. Burdock criticized or ridiculed him, he would tell him he was out of line and leave the room.

3. Michael also wrote a letter to Mr. Burdock. He stated that he did not appreciate Mr. Burdock's condescending comments and mannerisms and described how negatively they affected him. Michael also made a list of his own positive qualities which proved his worthiness to Mr. Burdock. He expressed how much he loved and cherished Mr. Burdock's daughter. Michael ended the letter with a

strong statement of intent: he wanted to get along with Mr. Burdock, but not at the expense of his own self-esteem. If the older man refused to accept Michael for who he was and could not treat him with respect, then Michael would sever the relationship.

Michael put this letter in an envelope, addressed it, and tucked it under some clothes in one of his drawers. He never did send the letter; knowing it was there was all he needed to cope with the insecurities he felt with his father-in-law. Michael saved the letter for two years before he threw it away.

Feeling prepared allows us to experience the power of choice. Our insecurities are often directly related to feeling completely helpless. We may have an all-or-nothing attitude in order to cope with our feelings of inadequacy. For example, if you are insecure about your weight, you may have emotionally trapped yourself in a corner—you are either fat or thin—nowhere in-between. In reality, most of us are in-between!

It is much healthier to view yourself as a person in progress. You may be heavier now than you'd like, but five minutes from now, you may be on the road to your ideal weight. Changing can make you a much more content human being.

We may be like oval eggs today. But exploring whatever negative feelings are holding us back and changing our attitudes toward them can make us a round circle.

Granted, there are some circumstances that cannot be changed: the death of a loved one, a bankruptcy, terminal illness, permanent handicaps, or a criminal record. These and other traumatic situations can't be erased. However, the way we choose to view these things and deal with them is totally within our power.

I was ten years old when my sister Laura Jean died. I felt so frightened and helpless. I developed a fearful insecurity that I would lose other loved ones, and when I had children of my own, I was hyper-vigilant about their safety. My interest payments were expressed through anxiety attacks and my need to steer circumstances that were beyond my control.

As I matured and made withdrawals from this particular account, I accepted the fact that I couldn't control everything in my life. Barbara Minar, a good friend of mine, and author of *Unrealistic Expectations* and *Close Connections*, gave me some very sound advice during an especially painful time in my life, "The only way around pain is to lean in and go straight through it."

How true. Either we can spend our lives fighting and avoiding our insecurities, or we can plunge in and pierce through their inner core. Eventually I faced the fact that I *will* lose loved ones and that there will be tragedies; however, my attitude can make these tragedies easier to cope with. If I try to escape the pain, I only prolong my anguish. But if I lean in and walk straight through the middle, I become stronger more quickly.

Our insecurities push us out of circle shape and keep us from completely enjoying the gift of life. We deserve to live free of their annoyance. It isn't necessary to live permanently as oval eggs. We can reclaim our round circles!

The following quiz will help you examine your records in order to find your personal emotional insecurities account. You will discover where you make deposits, how you pay interest, and how you can brainstorm to make withdrawals and close your account.

Quiz: Examining the Books

Circle **True** or **False** as the following statements apply to your personal life:

1. I don't like to entertain guests in my home.
       True   **False**

2. I think the end of the world is near.
       True   **False**

3. I feel jealous when my spouse talks to members of the opposite sex.
       True   **False**

4. I am embarrassed when my kids misbehave in public.
       True   **False**

5. I believe there are people at work who would discredit me to get my position.
       True   **False**

6. I worry about what would happen if I were laid off.
       True   **False**

7. I groom my lawn with great care.
       True   **False**

8. I am a miser; I stash pennies for a rainy day.
       True   **False**

9. I wish I measured up to the standards my partner has set for me.
       True   **False**

10. I am inconsistent in disciplining my children.
        True   **False**

11. I work late anytime I'm asked—even if it's inconvenient.
        True   **False**

12. I feel upset after reading the paper or listening to the news.
    True   **False**

13. I am critical of how I look.
    True   **False**

14. I've always wanted to have my own business, but I never have.
    True   **False**

15. I allow my kids to talk me into letting them do things—even after I initially said, "No."
    True   **False**

16. I buy things in surplus: clothes, linens, food, paper, and other supplies.
    True   **False**

17. I am uncomfortable telling someone my salary or the price of my house, car, or other large purchases.
    True   **False**

18. I worry that my spouse may have an affair.
    True   **False**

If you answered *true* to two or three in each group listed below, you may want to dig further and follow the steps outlined in chapter two to close your emotional insecurities account:

1, 7, and 13:   insecurity over appearances

6, 8, and 17:   insecurity over finances

3, 9, and 18:   insecurity about marriage

4, 10, and 15:   insecurity about parenting

5, 11, and 14:   insecurity in career

2, 12, and 16:   insecurity about the future

In each category you have insecurities, ask yourself the following questions:

1. What hurts do I have in this area of my life and how do I keep them alive? (Deposits)

2. How do these hurts show themselves through negative feelings or reactions? (Interest Payments)

3. What can I do to change my attitude about my hurts and the way I react? (Withdrawals)

4. How can I prepare myself for related situations in the future?

CHAPTER THREE
Circles in the Sand

Coming full circle and leaving dysfunction behind involves learning to protect yourself from the manipulations, demands, or requests of others that make you act and think in ways that bring negative results or pain to you. It means developing healthy barriers between you and harmful situations. It is fine to do things for others, but not to the point where it's detrimental to yourself.

Without protection, you are vulnerable to many kinds of negative influences; you will flip-flop and thump along as an oval egg instead of purposefully rolling forward as a round circle.

One protection system available to you is the creation of healthy personal boundaries. Imagine drawing circles in the sand around yourself. It is your job to be sure that nobody trespasses inside these circles. Every time you say, "No," to someone's inappropriate request, you draw a circle in the sand which creates a personal boundary.

Many of the hurts we experience as adults can stem from childhood situations in which we had no boundaries. We couldn't say, "No," and we had to rely on our caregivers to protect us. When these adults abused or neglected their authority, our circles were violated, and we had no defense. Therefore, we grew up lacking healthy personal boundaries which opened us to be abused or neglected.

It is vital to our well-being that we create and maintain boundaries—circles in the sand—around ourselves in order to have fulfillment and happiness. Let's look at two people who should have drawn personal circles in the sand.

Creating Healthy Boundaries

Susan cringed inwardly as her boss approached.

> He laid a paper on her desk and said, "Please do this letter before you leave the office. I'll be gone tomorrow, and I need to sign it tonight."

Susan looked at the clock. Four fifty-five. Greg would be furious if she got home late. He'd invited a client over and she'd promised she'd have a special dinner ready on time. The sitter would be irritated if she didn't pick the kids up by five-thirty. And she still had to bake the cake she said she would deliver for the preschool fund-raiser first thing in the morning. She should tell her boss she couldn't stay to do the letter.

> Susan took a deep breath, looked up at her boss, and nodded, "Okay, I'll have the letter on your desk in a little while."

Always something. This kind of day was not unusual for Susan; her life was very hectic. She has a hard time saying "No" to people. In other words, she does not place a very high value on herself and has trouble making choices that protect her self-esteem.

In Susan's case, her inability to say "No" has caused her a great amount of anxiety, guilt, and stress. Sound familiar?

If she is to balance her life and strengthen her relationships, she must learn how to set healthy boundaries. When she does this, others will be forced to respond to her new behavior and interact with her in more appropriate ways. For example, if Susan's boss frequently asks her to stay late—and this is not part of her job description—she may tell him that she cannot stay at the office today. By standing up for herself, she is setting a boundary that he has to deal with. He could react in anger or frustration, or he may choose to accept her stand and even suggest alternatives. Maybe the letter can actually wait, or Susan could sign it in his absence.

The major problem is that Susan needs to consider her own welfare. By setting a healthy boundary, she takes full responsibility for her own well-being. Further, if this *is* a constant issue at her office, Susan also forces her boss to be more responsible and to respect her needs.

On the other hand, if this is an unusual circumstance and Susan feels it is important to stay at the office and help her boss, she may then choose to call her husband and explain the situation. She could ask Greg to pick up the kids and order take-out dinner. There are always choices to explore and healthy boundaries to set.

As you initiate or restructure boundaries, you must be careful not to overcompensate. You may become so rigid in your new standards and ideals that you overuse your newly found power. It is wise to guard yourself from using your new freedom as license to be unfair or abusive to others.

For example, if Susan chose to defiantly say, "No!" to all the commitments she'd already made *and* to her boss's request, she would be doing herself, and those affected, an unnecessary injustice. She needs to consider the demands and decide which ones to accept and which ones to refuse.

It is vital that you take the time to think things through; consider your specific needs and discuss them with trusted others before making any abrupt decisions. You needn't attack those who you feel have burdened you with unrealistic expectations. Rather, carefully determine what boundaries are best for you.

And, yes, it is important to think about the well-being of others. It is impossible to live and work with other people without considering their needs, as well as your own. But by valuing others and yourself, you foster the opportunity to experience fuller, more meaningful relationships.

This is the key to setting appropriate boundaries and becoming a well-rounded person: Realize that the main goal must always be to change yourself—not the other person!

The balance in people's lives topples most often when they feel helpless to change anything. Susan is at this point. She needs to learn how to say, "No," when it is necessary for her own well-being.

Risking Disapproval and Rejection

Unexpected change can rattle even the most easygoing and well-adjusted person. Some changes can be as easy as going to bed an hour earlier; others can be as confusing and emotionally distressful as getting lost in a bad part of town. Here is one example.

Keith decided he was fed up with keeping his nose to the corporate grindstone; he'd done it for nearly twenty-five years. He was forty-eight years old and exhausted from the wear and tear of the lifestyle he'd previously chosen for himself.

Keith and Jillian were married right out of college and had three children by the time they were in their mid-thirties. Keith worked hard in business management and made a good living for his family. Jillian had a degree in communications, but the couple had decided she would remain at home to raise the children.

When Jillian announced that she wanted a divorce after twenty-five years of marriage, Keith was stunned. He knew that Jillian struggled with several disappointments and frustrations but had no idea how unhappy she'd been.

They tried marriage counseling. They tried to improve their sex life. They tried vacations along with everything else they could think of to make their marriage work. But it was hopeless; they were through. In the end, Jillian got a very good attorney and won steep alimony and child support payments. Keith was devastated emotionally and strapped financially. He was now paying for two households on the same salary.

Keith limped along in self-pity and despair for seven years before he looked honestly at the reality of his situation. He had followed the path he thought was right. He had provided a good life for his wife and children. What he hadn't done was care for his own inner needs or express his own natural personality.

He had allowed himself to try to fulfill the dreams of Jillian and their children. Keith had hardly set a single boundary for himself. If Jillian wanted new furniture, they got new furniture. If Jillian wanted to go back east for Christmas, they went back east. If Jillian wanted the family to eat health food, they ate tofu. Keith had acted like a robot, nearly forgetting the man inside who used to be excited about life. He had sacrificed his own dreams of a quiet, intimate life in a coastal fishing village for the jungles of suburbia—paying for a beautiful home, two nice cars, and braces for the kids' teeth.

For the past year, Keith had been searching his soul to find his dream, dust it off, and see how feasible it would be to pursue it now that he was in his late forties. His years in business management had given him a good sense of self-discipline; he didn't make hasty decisions in the passion of a moment. So he carefully composed a plan—just as he would do with any business proposal—to complete his dream. Then he considered it for several weeks:

- ○ Give up my apartment in Denver.
- ○ Sell my stocks and bonds for cushioning.
- ○ Cash in my retirement fund.
- ○ Discuss the plan with Jillian and the children.
- ○ Give half of my retirement money to Jillian.
- ○ Use the other half to start a business on Oregon's coast.

Keith's plan would put distance between him and his children, but would also lower his current financial obligations to his ex-wife.

He took his plan to an attorney. The attorney warned Keith that he could be in for a big battle. Jillian was not likely to give up her comfortable standard of living without a fight. She would probably attempt to convince the court that Keith had gone off the deep end or that he was trying to escape his parental responsibilities.

Keith gaped at his attorney, "You mean that my ex-wife actually has a chance to ruin my dream?"

"You can still have your dream, but you can't downscale the payment obligations you have to her and the kids, which you need to do in order to complete your plan."

Keith nodded. It was true. If he couldn't reduce his alimony payments to Jillian, he could survive only a few weeks after a move. Their oldest child was in college. The middle one would be a freshman next year. And the youngest, only fifteen, was still at home.

Keith knew he had several years of obligations left in rearing the kids. But Jillian was healthy. She had a college education. Why couldn't she at least support herself? Why should Keith sacrifice his happiness so that she could live a life of leisure?

Keith left the attorney's office feeling powerless. He truly believed he'd done the right things for the right reasons during his marriage. Now it seemed that Jillian's choices would dictate who he was for the rest of his life.

Keith grew despondent. For several weeks his coworkers watched him sink deeper into depression. One day his secretary finally had the courage to tell him what she saw as the truth of the situation.

> "Keith, I care about you. You've been a good boss and a good friend. It breaks my heart to see you roll over and refuse to stand up for yourself! I've watched you allow Jillian run over you with her incessant demands and her refusal to grow up and take responsibility for her choices. I think you are afraid of her disapproval and rejection."

Keith looked at his secretary and knew she was right. He'd never been able to protect himself in the face of Jillian's disapproval and judgment. He'd always given in to her. He now made a deep resolve—he would learn how to take control of his life!

During the next months, he joined a support group for divorced fathers. He drew great strength from hearing how others suffered through the same trauma he had faced. Keith began to open up; he expressed his feelings about how things had been, were now, and how he want them to be in the future. With the help of his new support network, Keith began to implement his plan to move west and start his life over.

The other men gave him courage to confront Jillian with his plan. They warned him that she would probably feel threatened and react very negatively. Keith approached Jillian feeling calm and sure of himself. However, *nothing* could have prepared him for her vicious attack. She raged for hours and accused him of being a disgusting male. She ridiculed his plan mercilessly and criticized him personally. She told him he was a loser, that he'd never made her happy, that he was the worst sexual partner she'd ever had, and that his parents had raised a mouse of a man.

Keith crumbled into a thousand tiny pieces. He felt completely rejected and shameful—he was a worthless piece of garbage. He reacted to Jillian's attack in silence.

> When she finished her tirade, he got up from the table, looked at her calmly and stated, "From now on, the only communication I will have with you is via our attorneys. Good-bye, Jillian."

Keith was shocked that his trembling legs could even move him to his car. But they did. And he immediately drove to the office of one of the men in his support group. As soon as the man shut the office door, Keith broke down and sobbed. For the first time, he allowed himself to feel his pain and grief.

However difficult it was, this was the release Keith needed to begin putting himself back together. Keith had drawn his first circle in the sand around himself, and it was a powerful one. Now he could truly discover and proclaim his own personality.

The Art of Proclamation

None of us arrives at our twenty-first birthdays with a piece of paper proclaiming who we are. Who we are is a dynamic, ever-changing process of maturing, discovering, and evolving. Healthy adults will proclaim who they are many times during their lives. We are not the same people at fifty that we were at twenty, thirty, or forty.

The art of proclamation is not violent or abusive. It is a delicate balance between creating healthy boundaries for ourselves and respecting those of others. Another's needs may not fit well alongside yours.

If you are my hair stylist, our differences don't really matter because we don't have much contact with each other. However, if you are my child's teacher, the situation becomes more complicated. You and I may have extremely different beliefs, lifestyles, and acquaintances, but I must learn to get along with you because you have my child in your care for much of the time. You have a major influence on my child's develop-ment of morals, beliefs, and skills. Therefore, I need to be certain my boundaries are clear to you, that I know and respect yours, and that you and I both take seriously my child's boundaries.

The art of proclamation involves communicating personal boundaries without blowing other people to pieces with the force of our desires. In fact, many times we can draw our circles in the sand without ever telling anyone. We can do this through . . .

    1. SELF-AWARENESS
    (Having a true awareness of our own needs)

    2. PERSONAL DISCERNMENT
    (Discerning how we can best meet those needs)

    3. INDIVIDUAL COMPREHENSION
    (Comprehending *why* these needs are important to us)

With this insight, I can proclaim to the world who I am. In other words, with *knowledge*, *wisdom*, and *understanding* I can master the art of procla-mation.

For example, I know that I need a lot of affection. I have the wisdom to discern that not everyone is like me and that I must take responsibility for surrounding myself with affectionate people in order to meet my needs. I cannot assume that other people automatically know my need for affection. Therefore, I take the initiative to give hugs, smiles, and pats on the back and, often, receive the same in return. In this way, I proclaim who I am without demanding aloud to those in my life, "I want you to hug me, smile at me, and pat me on the back when you see me!"

There's nothing wrong with articulating your needs; and many times this is very effective. But it's hardly feasible to tell every person you see what your personal needs are. The bank teller surely doesn't want to hear that I need a lot of affection to feel like a whole person. Yet when I smile at her and she smiles back, I am a bit fuller because of the exchange, and my needs are closer to being met for the day. When I thank the plumber for doing a good job—and he lights up—my needs are also met. When the doctor pats me on the back as I leave her office, we feel connected, and I feel more fulfilled.

There are times, of course, when we must proclaim our needs and boundaries much more overtly. These times usually become obvious with the onset of anger. Anger is the emotion that signals our inner selves that our needs are not being met or that someone has trespassed and violated our personal boundaries. Quite often we become angry because we have been tolerating behavior from others that goes against our own natural personality.

For instance, K.C. is a fairly sedentary person and quite content by herself. This does not always go over well with her very active and social husband, children, and friends. She used to feel guilty and inadequate because of this. She let herself be teased and coerced into doing many things she really didn't want to do. K.C. tried to live up to others' activity levels and expectations, but inside she was hurt and resentful.

Little by little, she deposited her negative feelings. The account soon became full, and interest was paid in the form of anger. Luckily, K.C. recognized and made withdrawals to close the account. She had not clearly proclaimed her needs to those who hurt her feelings. When she told them she needed more privacy and less activity, she raised a few eyebrows.

K.C. responded to the, "Come on, don't be so sensitive!" reactions by restating her position and saying that if she said "No" to a request, she expected to be heard and respected.

For a while some tried to relate in the same old ways to her. But she protected her circle shape and stayed true to her needs. Some worsened their badgering to the point of ridicule, trying to get her to react in the old, familiar ways. But K.C. stood her ground and was finally taken seriously.

She is now paid the respect she desires and has limited her relationships to those who honor and support her. K.C. saw that by allowing others to violate her boundaries, she had denied herself the right to be an authentic person. Her anger had signaled her to examine the imbalance in her life. Although anger can be unpleasant, it is an essential, protective emotion that we are wise to take seriously.

Proclaiming our personal needs to others can be a complex and risky process. None of us likes to be ridiculed or rejected. But the risk pays off in many ways: we are more comfortable with ourselves, we feel the strength and the power of freedom to be ourselves, and we expend more energy on our own productive growth.

Alecia knew what it was like to pretend she was someone who she wasn't. She was a hard-driving, thirty-something country-loving woman who had grown up with a demanding mother who had wanted a fragile and coy daughter.

Alecia endured her mother's attempts at reform until she was in her twenties. She took ballet lessons, went to the opera, and attended a young ladies' finishing school. She was finally introduced to society at a debutante ball. This occasion marked the beginning of the end of her mother's control. At the ball, she danced with another deb's father, Chas, who was a rancher in Montana. Chas and his ex-wife had divorced several years earlier, and his daughter was living on the East Coast where she had been raised by her mother. During her childhood, Chas's daughter traveled back and forth between the two parents, who led completely opposite lifestyles.

Alecia was fascinated by Chas's life in the West and questioned him at length for more information. The evening ended with Alecia wrangling an invitation from Chas to visit the ranch.

A few weeks later, Alecia tasted a kind of living that was delicious luxury to her. She enjoyed every minute of it. And, to her surprise, even though Chas was twenty years her senior, she completely enjoyed him, too.

Alecia returned to the East Coast and tried to go back to her former way of life. But she couldn't get Chas and his ranch out of her mind. She became depressed—and eventually physically ill—from trying to repress her true desires. Alecia's mother panicked. She did everything she could to get Alecia through her "phase."

Alecia secretly knew the source of her unhappiness, but she refused to risk her mother's contempt by revealing it. Then one night Chas telephoned and said he was in town visiting his daughter. He asked Alecia if she would like to go to dinner with them. Alecia's heart sang for the first time in months. Of course she would!

When Chas picked her up in a taxi, his daughter wasn't with him. She'd gotten the flu and stayed home. Inwardly, Alecia was thrilled. She soaked up the pleasure of the evening like a neglected house plant absorbing much-needed water. She sparkled.

When Alecia came home that night, her mother stared at her intensely. She wondered what it was about Alecia that was so different. Alecia acted as if she were in love with that farmhand! Alarms rang. Within a couple of weeks she had lined up a European trip. She would dazzle that lovesick look right off Alecia's face! If Paris didn't do it, then surely Rome would.

Alecia again went along with her mother's plans, but when she returned, she purchased a plane ticket, flew to Helena, Montana, rented a car, and drove to Chas's front door. She confessed her feelings for him and for the ranch life.

Chas was astounded by Alecia's revelation. He was also flattered and had to sternly remind himself not to fall into a relationship with her in her hysterical state of mind. He offered to let Alecia stay in the ranch guest house on the condition that she would take a week just to wander the countryside and think through her situation.

Alecia did this. She spent days riding horses, hiking, swimming in the creek, and pondering her life. She was very grateful to Chas for not taking advantage of her when he could have so easily. Alecia had tried to fit into the mold her mother cast for her. Without any healthy boundaries and a deep shame about her real needs, Alecia had tolerated her mother's abuse. But eventually she could stand it no longer. She made up her mind that she was going to confront her mother and tell her she was going to move west whether she liked it or not.

Alecia's mother did *not* like it. In fact, she has hardly spoken to Alecia in six years. But Alecia is fulfilling her true needs. She has a small working ranch of her own and is a close neighbor of Chas's. She's engaged to be married to the man who owns the feed store she patronizes and is content and hopeful about her life.

The breach in her relationship with her mother is a source of pain for Alecia. But she's learned, as we all must if we're going to be fulfilled individuals and live in our very own circle shapes, that she had to choose a lifestyle that allowed her to "come into her own."

Making choices to come full circle and be our true selves can be an extremely difficult task sometimes. But if we don't see to the tasks involved, we may be committing our own slow suicides. How others choose to react to our choices is their business.

Coming into Your Own

Once you've faced the ghosts from your past, the fears and insecurities of the present, and learned to create healthy boundaries for yourself, you are more than halfway to coming into your own. Now you can look in the mirror, see your true self, and know that you are growing up and paying your dues—and that life is showing you some amount of respect, however minimal. It's time to celebrate!

You know you've come into your own when . . .

○ You've dealt with your personal shame and worked through any blame you hold against others.

○ You've faced the fact that hindsight isn't always 20-20 and that you alone are responsible for examining any old patterns that haunt you.

○ You've made a commitment to contend for your own special niche in the world and to make your choices count.

○ You've examined the books of your emotional insecurities account, realized where you've made deposits, looked at the interest payments, taken the steps necessary to make withdrawals, and prepared yourself to deal with future insecurities as you closed your account.

○ You've defined your personal boundaries and learned to draw circles in the sand to protect yourself.

○ You've chosen to risk the disapproval and rejection of others as you learn the art of proclamation.

○ You've chosen to be true to yourself and risked revealing your real needs to at least a few others in your life.

As a result, you see a sort of transformation in yourself. You feel more self-acceptance and love. Even though no person is ever a finished product, you have taken the steps necessary to come into your own.

Now you are ready to deal with your relationships with others. You know how to get and keep your own circle shape. When circumstances pressure you into an oval, you know what to do to get back to your healthy inner circle. You have learned how to come full circle and have hope in the future.

If you are one of the millions who have chosen to be part of a committed relationship and in a family, then you are probably anxious to go on to the next area of circle connections: Couples—The Power Circles.

First, however, take a few moments to read over the "Suggestions for Loving Yourself" on the following page. You may find some helpful tips and refreshing information to aid you in maintaining your self—the inner circle.

Suggestions for Loving Yourself

1. Sit in a comfortable chair or lie on a bed. Close your eyes. Take a few deep breaths. Visualize yourself snuggling into a thick, fluffy cloud and floating in the sky with sunshine washing over you at just the right temperature. Allow yourself enough time to really feel the experience—the lightness of floating, the warmth of the sun, and the security of the cottony cloud wrapping you in its softness.

2. If you are not involved in a physical fitness program and your health allows it, take several seconds each day to simply jog or jump in place fifty times. You can do this while you are on the phone or just before your shower. Over a period of time, increase the number of jogs or jumps to one hundred.

    If you are already active in a fitness program, alter it. Change the who, what, when, where, or how of your activities to add motivation and zest to your routine.

3. While you bathe, or as you settle in to go to sleep for the night, silently repeat to yourself, "I am worthwhile and lovable." Affirmations such as this go into your "mind bank" and come out as dividends of more positive attitudes and behaviors. They recondition you mentally over a period of time and become an integral part of who you are.

Part II

Couples—The Power Circles

This

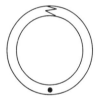

Not this

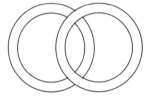

CHAPTER FOUR

Arcs of Love

Felicia and Rich were married shortly after they graduated from college. Like most couples, they went headlong into the union carrying their individual hopes, dreams, and expectations. They fully believed that "attaching their circles (themselves) together" was the means to their future happiness.

However, only a few months into their marriage, the signs of unrest that are common to many relationships began to emerge. Felicia did not feel cared for by Rich. Rich did not feel supported by Felicia. They became defensive with each other and bickered constantly.

Although fighting is common in new relationships, it is a red flag that tells us we need to pay more attention. Our national epidemic divorce rates could be bettered if we heeded early warning signs. If we can learn to promptly resolve our problems with our partners, we can avoid having to "clean up our mess" later.

I discovered this three years ago as I was preparing to write this book. You may recall that I keep personal journals. When I went to these for information, I discovered the basic problems that currently existed in my marriage were the same ones that had existed nearly two decades earlier! I began to ask others about their relational problems and discovered that the patterns were perpetual: Early relational problems evolve into long-term poisons if they are not resolved!

Why don't we solve problems that surface in the early days of our relationships? Surely we can feel and see the pain they cause. Why wouldn't we just spontaneously take care of them? One of the biggest reasons is that we have "attached" ourselves to our partners. In order to resolve our problems satisfactorily, we must pull back and look at our unique situations—we need to evaluate with some distance.

In fact, this chapter is titled "Arcs of Love" because attaching ourselves to our partners—like two metal rings soldered together—is unhealthy. It is better for us to keep our "arcs" connected only at one end. We should leave the other end loose in order for us to separate from our partner for activities, career development, or friends. This way we can connect and separate, be together, and be apart, as our own needs require while maintaining a healthy relationship with our partner.

Think of it in terms of rings on a three-ring binder; they never come completely apart. They are simply opened and closed as needed, according to the thickness of paper being bound.

In other words, when we commit ourselves to our partners, we agree to "arc together." But we should also be aware that we are different people; there will be many times when we must open the binder rings (without ever fully separating them) so we can take care of our individual selves.

Think, for a moment, about two rings that are connected like links of a chain. If you pull on the rings hard enough they will bend into oval shapes. They will still be attached, but they are no longer circular. However, if you pull on a binder ring, it simply separates. When you put it back together, it will always return to its original shape. This is how I see healthy partnerships.

But why are there so many unhealthy partnerships today? Why does the committed love relationship that so many millions of us seek cause so much pain and frustration? The answer lies in the fact that we incorporate our hopes, dreams, and expectations into our relationships instead of incorporating them into our individual selves. We want to fulfill ourselves through our relationships rather than through ourselves.

How You Learned to Be a Partner

Most of us learned how to act in committed love relationships in primarily two ways:

1. We observed our parents and other caregivers, with all their human frailties and dysfunctions.

2. We fantasized while watching television, listening to love songs, and reading fairy tales and romance novels (with no frailties or dysfunctions).

What a lethal combination! Reality and fantasy seldom coexist successfully. No wonder so many of us are disappointed when our relationships do not evolve as we had planned. Reality and fantasy blend and weave throughout our lives, leaving us so confused about what to expect and how to go about things that most of our relationships are oval instead of circular.

Consider Ward and June Cleaver from the "Leave It to Beaver" television show or Mike and Carol Brady from "The Brady Bunch." Their so-called marital and family problems were presented, confronted, and resolved in less than thirty minutes of script. Fantasy. In reality, our problems can take years to resolve or never be resolved. And, as pointed out before, problems that are not resolved can be poisons that destroy our partnerships—and our lives.

We all know that we have been affected by love songs, fairy tales, and romance novels. The power of the music industry has influenced entire generations of people. Almost everyone has a fantasy of "the right person" coming along to save him or her from the cruel, cold world; that has been fed by popular romance novels. Do you really think that you will meet a gorgeous lover on a plane to Paris, get married in London, and both settle into careers as famous movie stars? It's doubtful.

Fantasy can, at best, offer us temporary escape from a world that is full of harsh truths. It can't, however, replace realistic expectations of our relationships. In learning to be healthy, partners must look for balance between reality and fantasy.

Perhaps many of us were driven, as children, to bury ourselves in fantasy because the reality of our home lives was so unpleasant. There was no allure in watching our parents toil, struggle, and fight to keep their marriage and family together. What we did enjoy watching were the parents on television. They rarely fought and were always loving and lighthearted. Little did we know the damage we were causing to ourselves.

DeDe is forty-one, divorced, and remarried. Her father worked for an auto manufacturer, while her mother took care of DeDe, her two sisters, and her brother. DeDe says:

> "I did not, and could not, understand how difficult their daily lives were. I can't imagine the amount of discipline it took for my dad to go to the same job every day for thirty years just to keep a roof over our heads and food on the table.

> "And my mom—I almost blush when I see the sacrifices she must've made so my sisters and I could have the prom dresses we thought we deserved and our brother could be in all his extracurricular activities.

> "You know, at the time I thought my parents were the most boring, straight-laced people in the world. Now I realize that they are the most wonderful, exciting couple I know. I appreciate their stamina and character and their loyalty to each other throughout the years. This kind of caring and commitment cannot be reduced to a half-hour sitcom or a three-minute love song. You have to experience it yourself to really grasp the importance of it all."

DeDe's right. Reality cannot be reduced, condensed—or denied. No matter how hard we try to hide in pleasure-of-the-moment entertainment, reality always comes back to find us. We must be open-minded "students of life" to learn how to be good partners. What if we did not have good role models? What if one or both of our parents were abusive, mentally ill, or frequently absent? With the abundance of pain, is it any wonder that we tried to soften our disappointment with fantasies?

Although this explanation excuses us from not having learned how to be good partners, it doesn't excuse us from taking responsibility and learning healthy relational roles. In order to get beyond dysfunction we must see the force behind our behaviors: Our driving motives are getting our basic emotional needs met.

Whether we had good role models in childhood, like DeDe, poor ones in reality, or false ones in fantasy, we will always seek to get our needs met.

Powerful Needs

Lloyd John Ogilvie, in *God's Transforming Love*, says our undeniable emotional needs are . . .

- ○ To be loved.
- ○ To feel forgiven (accepted "as is").
- ○ To experience security.
- ○ To sense adequate hope for the future.

These resonate as accurate and true. If you have any negative feelings in your life, you will be able to trace them to one or more of these unmet needs.

Whether your parents taught you healthy or unhealthy ways of relating, you will instinctually do what you must in order to have your basic emotional needs met. If fantasy helped you meet your needs as a child, that's fine. But you are an adult now, and it is imperative to your well-being and to the success of your relationships that you choose to live in reality.

Remember this as we discuss this issue further: Regardless of how dysfunctional your family of origin was (or is), you will subconsciously equate their actions with your present-day reality.

This is where the circles of reality and fantasy may have become linked. When reality felt awful during your childhood, you may have consciously decided you wanted no part of it.

So you perhaps latched on to fantasy to create a mental picture of how you wanted your adult life to be. Unfortunately, this can be very detrimental to your potential happiness because fantasy is exactly that—a mental image that is not real.

Take Celia for instance. She grew up in a home in which her father was terribly abusive and manipulative. He bullied his wife and children into doing his will. Celia then married Thomas, who was raised by a whiny and selfish mother. The reality at home for Celia and Thomas was less than ideal. Each person had unique fantasies of how a happy couple should act but no skills to turn those fantasies into reality.

When Celia and Thomas got married, they brought their separate realities and fantasies to their marriage. Now their circles were doubly linked! Celia thought of men as bullies with ulterior motives for every action. Thomas thought of women as weak and self-serving. Celia fantasized about marrying a gentle and caretaking man, while Thomas fantasized about marrying a strong and benevolent woman.

You can easily see they were headed for trouble. The realities did not come close to matching the fantasies. Neither fantasy nor reality was healthy. Celia and Thomas had to back off, separate their arcs, and examine each of their pasts, hopes, and expectations together.

After discovering the source of their problems, they then set new goals for themselves and for their marriage. In order to have a powerful circle in their relationship, they needed to start over. First, Celia observed her father's ways. She realized that not all men manipulated women through abuse and bullying. Thomas certainly didn't. She realized that he was not motivated by "what he could get from her." It was perfectly normal for him to have expectations of her, as long as he didn't use force like her father.

Thomas studied the role his mother had played in his life. He saw that, although Celia was a strong and giving person, she would still have moments of weakness and needs of her own; she was completely normal.

Celia and Thomas then shared their fantasies and devised ways to have a realistic, healthy marriage. They clarified their basic, emotional needs and thought of how they could meet their own needs and each other's. To help them sort their thoughts, they each made a chart on paper. Tom and Celia's sample charts are on the following page.

Celia Feels . . .	When . . .
Loved	Told; praised; invited to lunch; given thoughtful presents; asked how I am; helped with chores or problems; and offered empathy
Forgiven/Accepted	Told; friends and loved ones are willing to be around me even if I've made a mistake, behaved badly, or don't feel my best; and when asked for my opinions and preferences
Secure	Hugged; bills are paid; housework is caught up; groceries bought; snuggling on sofa with Thomas; my job is going well; and I'm healthy
Hopeful	Encouraged by friends; supported by loved ones; I have a trip or event to look forward to; I'm able to save money from my checks; weather is nice; and I'm going to church

Thomas Feels . . .	When . . .
Loved	People do things for me; tell me they love me; hug me; invite me places; and show concern through calls or visits
Forgiven/Accepted	People trust me with personal information; I'm given special assignments at work; Celia makes a special meal; and others approve of me or my performance
Secure	Bills are paid; money's in savings; no threat of job loss; at home in front of a fire on a stormy night, cuddling with Celia
Hopeful	There's something to look forward to; plenty of work; things are in harmony at home; I'm meeting my goals; have plans with Celia; and when Celia and I laugh together

Celia and Tom then exchanged lists. They considered them seriously and realized that they had many things in common and that they must be more attuned to each other's needs and desires.

This is an excellent exercise for any couple needing to see where past realities are invalid and present fantasies are harmful. Try doing this with your partner, but be sure to be completely open and honest with your answers.

Celia and Thomas are like most of us; they were drawn to each other in the timeless quest for true love to unite them into a complete circle. There seems to be a compelling desire to "become one" with another. This is perfectly natural, and, in fact, a spiritual need for most people. But great care must be taken to "arc" together instead of "link" together.

Completing the Circle

The couples who "link" together usually find their realities frustrating, at best, and devastating, at worst. People cannot depend solely on one another to make their lives whole. They must commit to being responsible for their own selves and arc together to complete the circle shape of their partnership.

Esther and Gerald are an example of a couple who have had a lasting, successful marriage. They are in their early seventies and have been married for nearly fifty years. When they first married, however, they were out of sync with other couples their age because Esther continued to teach school after their honeymoon. This was unheard of in the early forties. When a woman was married, she usually gave up her personal ambitions and became a homemaker for her husband and children. But Esther and Gerald decided that what was best for others was not always best for them. Esther loved teaching and hated cooking and farming. Gerald was at his best when he was plowing the fields and making beef stew for dinner.

Esther and George made a deal. She would continue to teach, while he farmed the land. She would tend to the housework before and after school, and he would prepare and serve the meals. By combining their individual needs and preferences, they both felt fulfilled, emotionally secure, and loved.

When Esther had their first child, she and Gerald decided that it would be best for her to resign from full-time teaching. Instead, she tutored students in her home and did substitute teaching when needed. On days when she taught, Gerald cared for the baby. He also watched the baby on other occasions so Esther could have some free time. And she did the same for him.

Esther and Gerald had two more children. They raised them as a team. They worked side by side and lived a reality that many would envy. They were two arcs that separated when necessary without ever breaking their permanent bond.

In 1968, Esther and Gerald's eldest, a daughter, demonstrated with thousands of other college students and spent a night in jail. Esther and Gerald refused to bail her out; they said she must learn to pay the consequences of her actions. A few months later, their eldest son was killed in the Vietnam War. Esther and Gerald still clasp each other's hands and get teary eyed when they think of his death.

In 1969, Esther and Gerald's younger son was so devastated by his brother's death that he tried to commit suicide; he spent several weeks in a psychiatric hospital eighty miles from home. Esther and Gerald drove to and from the hospital three times a week to assist him in his recovery.

Their lives have not always been easy—or been like a fantasy. But Esther and Gerald are still happily together because they've learned how to live in their own reality. They are resilient.

How to Be Resilient

To master the art of resilience, you must learn to be like a sponge—you may be soaked full of water and squeezed to death, but you must eventually spring back to your original form and let the water evaporate. Couples who have overcome harsh realities in life repeat the same sponge-like patterns when they demonstrate resilience. They . . .

    ○ Accept their present circumstances.
    ○ Are willing to let time pass.
    ○ Know that things do change with time.
    ○ Do the best they can with the resources they have.
    ○ Allow friends and family to love and support them.
    ○ Have faith in God or a higher power.
    ○ Hope for a better future.
    ○ Pursue interests outside of themselves.

For some couples, developing resilience has included growing closer together. For others, it has meant therapy, changing careers, moving, hiring help, or altering lifestyles. There are no uniform answers. Each of us must try, by trial and error, to find the specific things that help us become resilient.

Esther said she and Gerald had to get rid of their unrealistic expectations in order to be resilient.

> She said, "Unmet expectations give you excuses not to be happy with what you have, who you are, or who you're married to. I thought about this for a long time—the more I though abut it, the more I saw its truth. The expectations that we have of others cannot possibly be met all the time. Therefore, we only set ourselves up for heartache when we cling to them.

> "For example, I know that as a young wife, I held on to the fantasy that my husband would fulfill all my needs. I expected him to be kind, courteous, considerate, and loving. I naively thought if he loved me enough, I would be happy and completely satisfied. When he did not fulfill this impossible request, I was greatly disappointed. I thought there was something wrong with me because he was not living up to my expectations.

> "Then the shame-and-blame cycle began: If I tried just a little bit harder, waited a little bit longer, did the right things, said the right words, cooked the right meals, and so on, he would act the way I expected him to, and in turn, I would be happy.

> "When this still did not work, I became angry, resentful, and full of self-pity. I would not be denied my 'right' to happiness! Why wouldn't my husband be who I wanted him to be? And why couldn't he see how easy it was to make things 'perfect' between us?

> "Groan. Groan. Groan. Something was very wrong, and after years of education, experience, and research, I realized what was keeping me from being happy: I was codependent."

CODEPENDENCY Instead of INTERDEPENDENCY

In her book, *Facing Codependence*, Pia Mellody gives five symptoms of codependent people. They have difficulty with . . .

1. Experiencing appropriate levels of self-esteem.
2. Setting functional boundaries.
3. Owning and expressing their own reality.
4. Taking care of their adult needs and wants.
5. Experiencing and expressing their reality *moderately*.

That was me, too. I was a young wife and a young mother. I was unsure of myself. I did not know how to set boundaries. I did not know what my own reality was. I expected my husband to take care of all my needs and wants. And I made it an all-or-nothing proposition. If my husband was not going to be everything I wanted him to be, then I would not be happy with my marriage.

Moderation was not something familiar to me at the time. Actually, I was not consciously familiar with any of these concepts. I was a true-to-form victim of the reality-versus-fantasy syndrome. And it would be a long haul to find my circle shape.

First, I had to look to my self—my inner circle. I had to work through the issues addressed in the first section of this book. Then I had to unlink myself from my husband and realize I was a separate person. Like binder rings, we needed to be joined at the base, not completely linked together. This realization necessitated long periods of struggle between codependency and interdependency. Even when we know that something is better for us, it often takes time and a lot of patience until we accept and embrace it.

The next step was to join my husband in a true, resilient power circle. It is much easier now when the need or desire arises to separate our arcs, step back, examine a problem, and take responsibility for our individual selves and our mutual relationship.

Many couples are like two eggs plunking around on a table. If one spouse falls off or the two crash together hard enough, one or both will break. This leaves a big mess that eventually has to be cleaned up. If we

make too many messes, we spend so much time cleaning up after ourselves that we do not get beyond destructive behaviors to practice
resilience and interdependence.

Before your partnership can become circular, it is vital that you each . . .

○ Review your pasts and examine how you learned to act in committed
   love relationships.

○ Release the fantasies you cling to.

○ Acknowledge and devise a plan to meet your basic emotional needs.

○ Consider what it means to be mutual partners.

○ Think of better ways to unite and separate from your loved one
   when necessary.

○ Explore incidents from your past when you were and were
   not resilient—how were the circumstances different or alike?

○ Eliminate unrealistic expectations you have for your partner.

○ Deal with any symptoms of codependency you may portray.

○ Be determined to form your own inner circles and become a
   healthy arc that comprises half a power circle.

Let's go back to your childhood when you probably learned how to be a
partner. The exercise that follows will help you see the areas where you
incorporated your realities and fantasies.

Exercise: Mapping Your Motives

List things you learned about relationships from your parents or others—good or bad.

1. _____
2. _____
3. _____
4. _____
5. _____
6. _____
7. _____

Now list fantasies you picked up from books, movies, or songs.

1. _____
2. _____
3. _____
4. _____
5. _____
6. _____
7. _____

Where Does Your Past Lead You?

Consider the things you listed above and ask yourself the following questions:

1. What can I do to be more realistic about my expectations of my partner?

2. What have I learned from others—especially my parents—about being in a committed relationship that I need to change?

3. In what ways were my parents happy?

4. In what ways were they unhappy?

5. How tightly do I cling to my fantasies?

6. Do I allow my fantasies to keep me from growing and enjoying a healthy relationship?

7. Do I use my fantasies as an excuse to blame my partner for disappointments I may have?

8. Do I need to be more flexible about my expectations of myself, my partner, and our relationship?

After completing this exercise, you should have a good idea of what you need to do: reevaluate and change unhealthy conceptions of reality and idealistic fantasies.

In the next chapter, we will look at negative influences that affect our relationships. We will see how these influences can destroy the relationship we most want to succeed and then learn how to defend ourselves from those influences.

Chapter Five
When Love Feels Like Handcuffs

When you feel you are handcuffed to the person you love and also feel hatred, anger, and contempt toward him or her, you naturally start to resent your partner. Just as there is tremendous positive power in a healthy relationship, there is equally negative power in the linked ovals of an unhealthy one.

Sometimes divorce or permanent separation is the only resolution. I am not encouraging these ideas, but sometimes they're the only solution. This is difficult for me to say—I would like to believe that it is always possible to work things out. But I know that both people must be mutually committed and respectful to maintain a successful relationship. Sometimes only one person is committed to making the marriage work. The most effective way to solve problems is to have the cooperation and willingness of both partners.

To do otherwise under these circumstances would be shorting yourself. Of course, there are some people who choose to stay in relationships like this. They subjugate their basic human needs to those of their partners. These are often the people who are so depressed and uptight that they often worry to the point of illness or premature death.

Our core selves are very resilient if we allow them to be, and they can often withstand much more pressure than we think. For example, if you are presently staying in a relationship for any of the following reasons, you may actually be subconsciously protecting yourself from rough waters. If you tough out the storm, however, you will end up on a calm, smooth sea. Are you staying in your relationship . . .

○ For the sake of the kids?
○ For financial comfort?
○ For religious reasons?
○ Because of personal fears?
○ For any reason other than love, respect, mutuality, commitment, or trust?

If you recognize yourself in this list, then you must:

1. Stop!
2. Think!
3. Face reality!
4. Get help to resolve your problems!

But let's suppose that the problems are not to the point of separation. Or let's assume that any challenges you do have are caused by external pressures, internal confusion, misunderstandings, or an inability to solve problems. Let's say that you and your partner are determined to mold the oval eggs of your relationship into a power circle of joined arcs.

If this is your situation, you are lucky because your problems will be easier to resolve. Use these four steps to stop for a moment, think about what is bothering you, face the reality of the situation, and get help from a trusted counselor or friend.

Pushing and Pulling

If you're feeling handcuffed to your partner, then you have likely experienced the push-and-pull of wants or needs. Beth and Randy know the feeling well. Beth explains:

> "A few years ago, Randy decided he wanted to change careers. He'd worked for the same company for ten years and had a chance to have a management position with another

company. But it seemed like he decided overnight to quit his corporate job and move several hundred miles away to open a mom-and-pop restaurant. All I could think of was the problems this would cause. We have two kids to consider. I have a good job, and our mortgage payments are low. Nothing about Randy's proposition made any sense!

"I was completely shocked, scared to death, and adamantly against the whole thing. This made Randy angrier than I'd ever seen him. He would not listen to a single negative comment about his plan. We began pushing and pulling each other until we could no longer stand it.

"One day, after more than two years of this tug of war, I told Randy, 'If you leave your job and follow through with this crazy scheme, I will leave you!'

"The whole thing reminds me of two kids pulling on opposite ends of a toy they want. At some point, one child gives way, the other falls on the floor, and the toy lies there, smashed to pieces.

"That's what happened when I gave Randy the ultimatum. I let go of my end of our marriage, he fell backward, and our marriage was left shattered on the floor. He turned stiff and told me that if that was what I wanted, I could pack my things and get out.

"I couldn't believe my ears. I looked into his eyes and knew that he meant what he said. Fourteen years of marriage—and he was willing, in that moment, to throw it all away for what seemed to me to be an illogical career change.

"I had begged him all those months to negotiate the situation logically with me. I made all kinds of suggestions: he could go to a career counselor, work nights at a restaurant to see if he even liked the business, or talk with people who owned restaurants to get first-hand information about the realities of it."

As I listened to Beth tell her story, my mind raced: What would I do if I were in her shoes? How could they possibly work this out? How can any couple survive such a no-win situation? Here is what they did:

> "When I realized that Randy was completely miserable in his current job and that he was willing to risk our marriage to find a new one, I made a fast assessment of the situation and told him, 'If you feel this strongly, then I want a few days to think things through and make some decisions of my own. I will let you know by the end of the week what I decide.'
>
> "I could see the expression on his face change from stubborn determination to relief to fear—all in a few seconds. I was scared to death, but I knew I had to follow through and let my instincts guide me. I left the room, and for the next four days, I searched my own soul like never before. Then I went back to Randy with specific guidelines."

These are the personal boundaries Beth set with Randy.

1. She reiterated that she was still against Randy's career change.

2. She shared her feelings about the situation, not about Randy. She was careful not to judge Randy and not to accuse him of being responsible for her unhappiness.

3. She restated the logical reasons against his plan and repeated the feasible alternatives.

4. She told him in a calm, clear voice that if he chose to proceed with an all-or-nothing course of action, she would take steps to separate from him.

5. She then emphasized that she did not want a separation and that her goal was to stay married and fulfill both their needs.

6. She said she would rather start over and devise a way for Randy to change careers without putting so much on the line.

7. Finally, she asked Randy to tell her his intentions by the end of the week.

Randy reacted bitterly. He accused Beth of not caring for him or his happiness. He began to ridicule and criticize her unfairly. Beth told Randy she would not stay in the same room and allow him to rave at her for disagreeing with his sudden career change. She quietly got up and left the room. As she walked outside to work in her flower beds, she heard Randy fussing and fuming in the kitchen.

The next week was a nightmare. Randy was irritable and sniped at Beth at every opportunity. At times, she was tempted to blow up and throw every self-righteous bit of anger in Randy's face, but miraculously she held her tongue. She knew inherently that doing this would only give Randy the justification he needed to blame her for the entire situation.

Instead, she kept quiet and went about her daily routine. This forced Randy to face his anger alone and to deal with his problem head-on. He remained surly and unapproachable the whole week. There were times when Beth thought she couldn't tolerate another minute.

Fear, Worry, and Anxiety

Beth's worry and anxiety grew each day until she felt her fears might soon overwhelm her. At one point, she felt so vulnerable she thought she was losing her mind. It was as if she were living a horrible dream; nothing seemed real anymore. Her mind filled with fretting questions: Could this really be happening to her? How would she ever manage to live without Randy? Would they get back together or find other lovers? She couldn't imagine them getting a divorce, yet her marriage was miserable.

Time dragged on as Beth robotically moved about as if nothing were different. She was not going to tell anyone else what was going on. She felt that the time would come soon enough if Randy barreled ahead with his plans. But two days before Randy was supposed to let her know his decision, Beth broke down in the break room at work. Between heaving sobs she told her story to Shelly and Lloyd, two of her coworkers. When she had finished, Lloyd, twenty years her senior, laid a hand on her shoulder and comforted her.

"Beth, I think you'll find that just getting this out into the open will help ease some of the fear and worry that you've obviously been holding inside. It seems like things in our minds are much more threatening if we keep them there instead of bringing them out to others."

Shelly, who was about Beth's age, also spoke with understanding.

"I know first-hand what it's like to worry myself sick about situations I had no control over. My father sexually abused me for years while I was growing up. I used to lie in bed at night and tremble with fear that he would come into my room and molest me."

Beth looked at Shelly compassionately, "Oh! I feel stupid for even complaining about my troubles. My goodness, you went through hell and here I am, worried that my husband might quit his job!"

Shelly responded quickly, "Don't invalidate your problems, Beth. I only shared that with you so you'd know I really do understand your feeling of helplessness. Your situation involves much more than Randy quitting his job. It means uprooting your whole family, leaving your job, and starting all over in an area where you know no one. That's not something to apologize for being upset about."

Shelly continued, "It took me many years to work through the effects of my father's sexual abuse. But one thing I know for sure is that you can't allow your anxieties and worries to prevent you from taking care of yourself. You need to look realistically at your circumstances and accept that there are some things you can't change. Of course, I wish I could change what my father did, just as I'm sure you wish Randy would change his mind. But I couldn't, and you can't. You have to let Randy make his choices and be prepared to follow through on your own."

Beth nodded, tears anew in her eyes. She knew that what Shelly said was true. It was just so hard to accept that Randy could be so self-centered after so many years of being a team. Beth needed to sort things out and, as Shelly said, be prepared to take care of her "self."

Confusion and Disappointment

For the next two days, Beth struggled with growing confusion. What were the right things to do? As a wife, should she "stand by her man" and go along with Randy if he insisted on having his way? He had a right to his life too, didn't he? And what about the kids? If Beth chose to stand her ground and Randy went off on his own, would the kids stay with her or go with him? What were their individual rights? There just weren't any specific rules to guide her through this situation.

Randy was not being a team player. She was sure that it was he who had betrayed their relationship. It was not her fault that Randy didn't like his job and was discontented. She liked *her* job. And, what if the situation were reversed? If Beth had decided the very same things and expected Randy to quit his job and move to a strange town so she could pursue a risky career, what would he do? Beth felt a small sense of excitement. She may have stumbled on a way to sort things through. She would put Randy in her shoes to show him how she felt.

She carefully thought this through and went over the scenario in her mind:

> She would tell Randy that she hated her job, wanted to quit, move far away, and open up a business in which she had no experience. This would necessitate Randy's trusting her to sink money from the sale of their home into the business. It would mean giving up full retirement benefits and cashing in on partial contributions from ten years of employment. It would mean Randy would have to find other meaningful employment, the kids would have to leave the only home they'd ever known, and they would have to lower their standard of living.

Beth didn't even bother to go on—she could see how ridiculous the whole thing was. Randy was expecting way too much of her and the kids. This was not the kind of marriage they wanted. Randy had to work this out personally. Beth then began to consider her own commitment to the marriage. At what point would she override her commitment to her marriage vows for her own self-gain? She didn't have to think hard about the answer.

On Saturday morning, Randy asked Beth if they could talk. Her heart began pounding. She nodded and followed Randy out to the patio with a cup of coffee.

> Randy cleared his throat, hesitated, and then blurted, "I gave two weeks' notice at work yesterday."

Beth felt a pounding in her head. Her heart thudded against her rib cage. For a moment she thought she might faint. Then she felt nauseous and ran for the bathroom to vomit. As she washed up and brushed her teeth, Beth looked in the mirror. Dark circles shadowed eyes that normally sparkled but now appeared hollow and tired. She began to think of what Randy's decision meant.

> Randy's voice interrupted her thoughts. "I'm sorry, Beth. I have to do it—for my own sake."

> Somehow, Beth collected herself. "Let me make sure that I understand you correctly. You gave your notice at work. You intend to put the house up for sale, move, and open up your own restaurant. And you are choosing to do this knowing my boundaries and the consequences?"

Randy nodded solemnly. Beth's face grew hot with rage. Her hands began to shake. She had never felt such hatred or resentment toward anyone in her life. He was really going to go through with it. The disappointment was so excruciatingly painful that Beth could not stand still. She brushed past Randy, grabbed her purse, and flew out the door. She started walking and kept on walking, unaware of where she was going or the tears that were streaming down her face.

Like so many before her, and many to follow, Beth was a casualty of a harsh realization: *what we think life is "supposed" to be like and what it really turns out to be is often completely different.*

In the end, Randy moved, leaving Beth and the children behind. Each spouse received half the money from their house. Beth bought a condominium where she lived with the kids. Soon after, however, Beth began to hear a great deal of remorse from Randy; he wanted to try to work things out.

Beth was faced with even more confusion. She still resented Randy and was not sure she could ever trust or forgive him. On the other hand, she never wanted to split up—life as a single parent was not fun. She was often lonely and depressed. She missed Randy's companionship and his help with parenting the kids.

Beth knew that if she forgave him, both she and the kids would have to move. All their money was tied up in his restaurant, which wasn't doing all that well, and in her condominium. How she wished, some days, that she could roll back the clock to a time when her biggest concern was what to make for dinner.

When I heard their story, my heart went out to Beth, the children, and to Randy. Obviously, Randy needed more than a new career. He needed to solve his personal problems and confusion before he could go on living with his family. The most difficult thing about these kinds of relational challenges is that each partner (arc) pulls away from the other; but they are still joined on the opposite side of their circle. This can cause great agony and grief.

For Beth and Randy, as is often the case in relational crises, things got worse before they got better. Beth decided to sell the condominium and move the family in with Randy. Although the sale went smoothly, Beth barely got her down payment back. She was leery of putting the funds into a joint account because Randy's business was still failing.

When Beth shared her feelings with Randy, he surprisingly agreed. He thought she was smart for putting the money away for her and the kids. Within six months the restaurant went belly up and the newly reconciled family found themselves in a dilemma that is common to many these days: middle-class poverty.

Middle-Class Poverty

There are few things that leave us feeling more anxious or vulnerable than financial struggles in these "Buy this! Buy that! You are what you have!" times. The most recent and hardest hit victims seem to be in the working middle class. The financial struggles Beth and Randy faced were further complicated by their personal situation. Randy shares his account of the situation:

> "I felt so guilty and ashamed of myself after I left Beth and the kids that I hardly took any pleasure in the restaurant at all. Who knows—maybe I subconsciously sabotaged myself as punishment for being such a jerk in the first place. But now it's even worse because every day I see Beth come home from work tired and sad. The kids are skittery and nervous a lot of the time. We used Beth and the kids' security money to pay off restaurant bills that otherwise would have gone into collection and forced us into bankruptcy. We figured if we filed for bankruptcy the kids would be grown and gone before we could hope to get another home loan.

> "At least this way we have a chance. Neither Beth nor I particularly care for our jobs. We each had to start over, and it will take us a while to get back to where we used to be—this is a rural community and there aren't as many high-paying jobs as there were in the city.

> "You can imagine how awful I felt, seeing Beth selling advertising for the local radio station when she used to take Fortune 500 executives to lunch on an expense account. The only job I could find was managing a frozen food warehouse—I'm way out of my league, also. I really made a mess of our lives, and I don't know what the future holds for us. I guess I wouldn't blame Beth if she left me."

I could hear serious depression throughout Randy's conversation. Yet, he was not seeing a physician or therapist for help. I asked him why.

> "We don't have health insurance and I can't afford it. I'm not going to take food out of my family's mouths after all I've put

them through. Besides, I guess I figure I deserve to pay for what I've done. But, man! What a price!

"For the first time in my life, I know what it's like to get shut-off notices from utility companies and collection warnings from creditors. I can't tell you how many times in the last year we thought our cars would be repossessed or we'd lose the roof over our heads. It's just plain nerve-wracking.

"I'd give anything for the days when Beth and I could fly to a ski resort for the weekend or send the kids to summer camp so we could be alone. It will be years, if ever, before we can enjoy those kinds of things again.

"At my former job, I had things like dental and eye-care insurance. Now we have neither, and one of the kids needs braces, which we can't afford, and the other needs glasses we will have put on our nearly maxed charge card.

"I'll tell you one thing, I have a lot more compassion for other people's troubles, and I don't pass judgment on them like I used to. It's very true—you can't understand why anyone behaves the way he or she does unless you know their situation or have experienced it yourself."

Seeing the pain on Randy's face made me realize that he really wasn't a bad person. Like many of us, he'd only made bad choices. The complications of these choices, however, brought dire consequences to himself and to his loved ones. As Randy learned, choosing to make radical changes within the family structure can have negative effects that last for years—and there's no going back. We can only, as mentioned in the first section of this book, lean in and pierce straight through the pain.

Leaning Into the Pain of Life

Beth chose to forgive Randy and to try making their marriage work under new, but very painful, circumstances. The money pressures were horrendous, of course, but for Beth, the emotional pressures were even worse.

She says,"It has been so hard for me to feel any love or warmth toward Randy. I feel self-righteous, and half the time I want to shout, 'See! If you'd only listened to me, we wouldn't be in this stinking mess!' But then I try to remember that Randy is living with his own regrets; he feels the same pain I do, only his is worse because he caused it. I don't want to rub it in his face, but I have a hard time letting go of my anger and bitterness!

"The financial pressures are driving us apart. We're tired, envious of our old friends who have financial security, and terribly frightened of the future. It is so awful to feel you can't provide for the basic needs of your children or make financial choices. And time is the only thing that offers any relief— time *will* pass and things *will* change, if we just hang on.

"There are many times when I feel neglected and emotionally unbalanced, but I make myself tough and remind myself that things will get better. I try to keep hoping that something wonderful will happen—one of us will get a sizable promotion or we'll be offered our old jobs. Who knows? Some days I feel so desperate, I hope I'll win the lottery.

"I sometimes think about leaving Randy and taking the kids back to where we used to live. Other times, I see how repentant he is, and I can't bring myself to consider leaving him. As you can tell, I'm still confused; I can't even describe my feelings because I don't know what they are. I worry now more than I did before we were separated.

"Ironically, I still take comfort in the fact that we're together. In fact, the only thing that keeps me here with Randy is our collection of photo albums. I look through them frequently and see our lives as they used to be—I just can't let go of it without a fight.

"I keep thinking that if one of our parents died, my best friend got cancer, or one of our kids got hurt, no one would know the pain I'd feel besides Randy. We've shared so much together. One brick of life at a time builds a whole house of history that can't ever be replaced. That collective history makes it worth fighting for.

"Even if we never regain financial standing, no one can take away our memories; and they certainly aren't all painful. Only Randy knows the little things that are funny to me— why I'm embarrassed in particular situations or why some of the comments my mom makes are so hurtful. I can never replace what we've shared together—having the kids, raising them, buying a house, being broke, and trying to work things out together."

Randy and Beth have a long road ahead of them. They seem to want to work things out, and they've certainly been creative in clinging to their tenuous circumstances. But what if your relationship isn't in such a turmoil? What if you just want to renegotiate the mental and emotional "rules" of your partnership? What if you want to create a "new" partnership from your existing one?

We'll discuss this concept in the next chapter. But before we go on, you may want to take the quiz that follows and consider the reality of your relationship. It is healthy to periodically take an honest look at, and assess, our lives so we can continue to live contentedly with our partners.

Quiz: Assessing the Damage

Choose the letter of the response that best describes you:

1. When I think about my partner, I feel:
      a) Warm and happy.
      b) Contemptuous.
      c) Angry and spiteful.
      d) Repulsed.

2. When I think about our relationship, I wish:
      a) I would have never committed to my partner.
      b) I would have chosen someone else.
      c) Others could be as happy with their partners as I am with mine.
      d) I would have done things differently with my same partner.

3. When I look back over the years I feel:
      a) Optimistic.
      b) Tired.
      c) Hopeless.
      d) Disgusted.

4. I hope my children:
      a) Take greater care than I did in choosing their partners.
      b) Consider not having a committed love relationship.
      c) Find as much happiness with their partners as I have with mine.
      d) Realize how depressing commitment can be.

5. Sexually, my partner:
      a) Completely turns me off.
      b) Is somewhat attractive.
      c) Is great in bed.
      d) Doesn't excite me as much as another partner could.

Assessment

If you responded . . .

1. a
2. c   You are extremely happy in your relationship, and you
3. a   know what it takes to have a mutual commitment with
4. c   a loving partner. Congratulations!
5. c

If you responded:

1. c
2. d   There is tension in your relationship that needs to be
3. b   eliminated. You could benefit from talking to a professional
4. a   about the trouble in your relationship.
5. b

If you responded:

1. b
2. b   You have lost respect for your partner and your future
3. c   together. You need to get professional help as soon as
4. d   possible. You'll be glad you did!
5. d

If you responded:

1. d
2. a   Your partnership is in trouble and has suffered severe
3. d   damage. Please, get help right away to start working
4. b   on salvaging your relationship.
5. a

You may have marked any combination of the above groups of answers. Maybe there is a particular area of your relationship that needs help. Or maybe you are going through an especially rough time personally right now. Above all else, be honest and follow your instincts when it comes to your relationship. Only you can decide whether you need help to unlock your relational handcuffs.

Chapter Six
The Promise of Undying Love

There is no relationship on earth that can have an energy so positive, a force so uplifting, or a meaning so privately intense as two people forming a round circle in a joyous partnership. On the other hand, there is nothing that can be as destructive, distressing, or utterly miserable as an abusive or unhealthy relationship.

If two people begin linked as round circles and begin to pull and push each other continuously, they lose their circle forms and become oval eggs. Many times, this battle arises from one or both people suppressing their feelings for long periods of time. If ignored long enough, a person's benign feelings may turn to anger, frustration, contempt, hostility, and despair.

If this sounds like your situation, I strongly suggest you seek professional help (if you are not already receiving it). It will be almost impossible for you to talk about your problems without an objective, trained third person. If your partner won't seek help with you, get it for yourself. Any move in a positive direction has merit, and you may be surprised at how a first move, such as going to therapy, serves as the first domino to fall in a line of others.

However, let's assume that both of you are aware of your problems and honestly want to resolve them. How do you start over? How do you renegotiate your relationship after so many years and create a life without destructive dynamics?

The methods that this couple used may be effective for you, too. After being together twelve years, Sarah and Ted had their biggest argument ever. They shot insults and accusations back and forth from evening until dawn. They were both miserable afterward. They lay in stony silence alongside each other in bed.

Ted whispered desperately, "Can't we start over, Sarah? Can't we just give ourselves a brand new chance?"

With this, Sarah burst into tears. In between sobs, she said, "I hope so, Ted. I'd really like to try."

They both had the willingness necessary in order to begin renegotiating their partnership. However, as with many others, it had taken a great deal of pain and an excruciatingly long time for them to "hit bottom." They would not resolve things overnight, but they had uncovered their first foundational building block:

1. WILLINGNESS

That morning, the couple fell asleep in each other's arms for the first time in weeks. They slept easily knowing that the day would finally bring hope to their relationship. But the day brought an unexpected tentativeness. Sarah and Ted were frightened to open up to each other—they'd burned each other one too many times to trust each other this soon.

Finally, Sarah said, "Look, let's commit to saving our relationship and promise to do whatever it takes to set things right between us later. We can only tackle one thing at a time."

Ted nodded. They now had the second foundational building block:

2. COMMITMENT

Ted thought a moment and said, "Why don't each of us list the problems that we feel are the most significant? If we accept that the other person's list is as important and valid as our own, then we can use the lists as our master plan for starting over."

Sarah agreed wholeheartedly. They had agreed that what was important to one of them would be important to both of them. The third foundational building block was in place:

3. MUTUALITY

Ted and Sarah each made a list of problems that threatened their relationship.

Ted	Sarah
Misunderstandings	Lack of communication
Sarah's criticism	Too little romance
Not enough time together	Ted's withdrawal
Sarah's lack of ambition	Lack of compassion
Sarah's mother and father	Ted's judgmentalness
	Unreal expectations

Ted and Sarah now had the fourth foundational building block upon which they could construct a new relationship:

4. DATA TO WORK WITH

Renegotiation can be seen as a pyramid of building blocks.

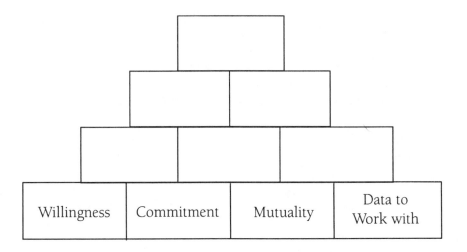

Ted and Sarah now have the foundation of their pyramid to happiness. As with any journey upward, the higher you climb, the more difficult it gets. Sarah suggested they use their combined data to develop realistic solutions. The fifth building block was in place:

5. REALISTIC SOLUTIONS

Ted and Sarah agreed to use the following tactics to improve their life together:

○ They would purchase videos or books that would help them develop better communication skills and lessen the number of misunderstandings they had.

○ They would take turns suggesting an activity they could do together once a week. By making this agreement and sticking to it, Ted would not feel so neglected by Sarah, and Sarah would be free to initiate more romance into their relationship.

○ They would think before they spoke to each other and practice saying positive things. This would break their habit of criticizing and needlessly tormenting each other.

○ Ted would try to say what was on his mind instead of holding his feelings inside. In exchange, Sarah would try not to criticize Ted, so he could feel safer to express himself.

Ted and Sarah felt the remaining things on their list were too immense to handle at this point. They were becoming wiser than they thought. Not everything can be resolved at once. Some things take a great deal of time and consideration to work through. Therefore, this is the sixth building block of the renegotiation pyramid:

6. BREAKING DOWN LISTS FOR MANAGEABILITY

Ted and Sarah broke their list down by creating the sub-lists for each problem that appear on the following page.

Ted	Sarah
Sarah's lack of ambition	**Ted's lack of compassion**
The house isn't tidy.	He isn't generous.
She won't strive for a promotion.	He acts superior.
She won't further her education.	He ridicules others.
Sarah's mother and father	**Ted's unreal expectations**
She jumps at their command.	He's a perfectionist.
They intrude on our privacy.	He tells me how to act and think.
They criticize both of us.	He's materialistic.

Trying to break down these issues caused some bitter arguments. Several times, Ted and Sarah had to separate their arcs and take time for themselves before they could rejoin their circle of renegotiation. One of the hardest things in renegotiating is working through issues that are defined by personal preference. Look at Ted and Sarah's lists again.

Who determines how tidy a house should be? Who determines whether a person is generous? Who has the right to tell others they don't strive enough, they need more education, they act superior, or they are too materialistic? This is where the seventh building block comes into play:

7. PERSONAL ACCOUNTABILITY AND ACCEPTANCE OF OTHERS

Ted and Sarah took a long look at their sub-lists. After many arguments, they finally realized that neither had the right to demand change from the other. For instance, Ted realized that if he wanted the house tidier, then he needed to do it himself and not impose his standards on Sarah.

He also admitted that it was not his right to tell Sarah she should strive for a promotion or further her education. Sarah pointed out that it was also not Ted's right to tell her how she should interact with her parents or to tell her how to act and think—he needed to accept her as she was.

On the other hand, Sarah realized she was wrong for judging Ted's generosity and materialism. She also needed to be accountable for herself and not impose her expectations on Ted. In addition, Sarah had to stop telling Ted that he was being a perfectionist; this was her definition, and she needed to accept him as he was.

Using this "relative barometer," Ted and Sarah were also able to agree that Sarah could not be responsible for her parents' behavior. She admitted that they criticized her and Ted too much, but she could not be accountable for how Ted handled the situation. Their definitions of criticism varied; therefore, they would have to discuss any criticism they received from Sarah's parents and deal with it together. They did agree, however, to support each other's opinions if her parents played them against each other.

Ted and Sarah were now left with two smaller issues to work out: Ted's ridiculing of others, and Sarah's allowing her parents to intrude in their private lives. These issues were not so relative because they were concrete. They tackled the ridiculing first. They decided that Ted would be more careful not to make comments that could hurt others—Sarah would give him a signal if he started to get out of line. She would not verbally chastise or embarrass him; rather, she would tap an index finger on her chin to warn Ted of his behavior.

Next, Ted and Sarah coped with her parents' constant intrusions. Fortunately, they were a step ahead with this problem: *they both put each other first*. Ted told Sarah he wished her parents would call and ask if they could stop over and respect their wishes if they said, "No." He also asked if she could decline some of the many invitations they received from her large extended family.

By this time, Sarah was feeling much less defensive and more benevolent toward Ted since they agreed to solve their problems. This made it easy for her to comply with his request. She approached her parents and tactfully laid out the new rules.

Because Sarah took care to be considerate in her assertions, her parents more easily accepted the new rules. They were somewhat stunned, but they also expressed regret for overstepping their bounds. They were very respectful of Ted and Sarah's wishes. Ted and Sarah were ready to move to the eighth building block:

8. PRACTICE

The couple got to a point where time and practice were the only things that could test their efforts. They agreed to take responsibility for their own parts during the next month.

After a month had passed, they sat down to assess their progress. This brought them to the ninth building block of the pyramid:

9. REEVALUATION

Periodically, it is important to gauge how far you've come in your re-negotiation and to discuss what is and is not working. You may find that resolving your larger problems will automatically unravel your smaller ones. It may be necessary to go through each building block of renegoti-ation several times as new problems arise or old ones resurface in order to put the top of the pyramid into place:

10. FINE-TUNING STUBBORN AREAS

There are bound to be issues that haunt you and are hard to solve. This is a fact of life. If you use the pyramid steps of renegotiation, however, you can handle problems that threaten your relationship.

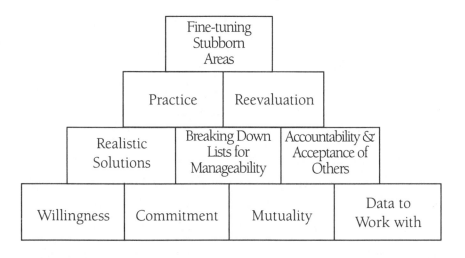

These steps will see nearly any couple through times of trouble. However, as I mentioned before, there may be such deeply rooted poisons in your relationship that professional help is needed. In these cases, the pyramid building blocks are excellent tools to aid in the process of your professional help. Once you and your partner have built your pyramid or gotten help, you must set personal limits.

Setting limits with your partner can be very difficult and confusing. Even if you have mastered "drawing circles in the sand," as discussed in chapter three, you may find that consistency is harder to maintain between you and your partner. One of the reasons for this is the vast number of influences encountered. We've learned from others what to expect, and from childhood on, we have absorbed attitudes and messages from 1) parents, 2) teachers, friends, and others, 3) religious organizations, and 4) society and the media.

When we enter a relationship, we bring to it everything we have learned and carry in our subconscious. Since there are two people involved, the information learned is doubled, and often not very similar. Therefore, each partner may have a multitude of learned behaviors and attitudes he or she is not even aware of that directly influence how he or she reacts to the other partner. This makes it very hard to set limits because we are dealing with more than what we directly see or hear.

For instance, this is a list of some commonly internalized messages and expectations:

O Good partners want sex often.
O Bad partners do not submit to their lover's desires.
O Good partners buy many gifts for their lover.
O Bad partners rarely surprise or romance their lover.
O Good partners take care of themselves and their looks.
O Bad partners are lazy and overweight.

You may find some of these generalizations to be true in reality or in your thoughts. Be warned, however, that they may complicate your relationship without you ever realizing it. The number of messages you absorbed that differ from your partner's messages will proportionately match how disappointed you are with you partner and the difficulty you have setting personal limits.

For example, in Lyddy's family, her mother was a full-time homemaker, and her father handled almost all the finances. He operated his own business and was the sole wage earner. For the most part, he alone decided how the money would be spent. Lyddy's husband, Gary, however, grew up in a completely different environment. His father and mother both worked, and his mother managed everything, including the finances. When they got married, Lyddy and Gary were unaware they had absorbed very different role messages.

> Lyddy's was, "A good husband makes the money and handles the finances for his family."

> Gary's was, "A good wife helps earn money and takes care of the family finances."

They had trouble for many years with this issue. Gary had no problem giving Lyddy his money or letting her manage it. She thought this was great at first—that it was a sign of his trust and respect. What she didn't know was that he also expected her to work and manage their money in the same ways his mother had.

Whoa! Lyddy anticipated being a full-time wife and mother and that was it. Now she was expected to get a job and handle the money. She couldn't handle all the responsibility. And without realizing it, Gary's subconscious had labeled Lyddy as a "bad" wife.

Conversely, Lyddy thought Gary would take care of earning and managing money. When this did not happen, she subconsciously labeled him as a "bad" husband. It took them a long time to figure out what was happening. They weren't happy with what they consciously decided to do. They had difficulty setting limits and defining responsibilities with each other because they were not aware of their subconscious desires; they both expected relationships like their parents'.

> It was very easy for Lyddy to set minor limits, such as, "I don't want you to wake me up early on Saturday mornings. I prefer to sleep in."

> And it was easy for Gary to say, "I don't want to dance when we go out because I don't like it."

It will be easy to set limits if you are aware that another person's actions cross your personal boundaries. But when their actions cross your subconscious boundaries, you cannot set limits until you discover what your subconscious desires or expectations are. Often a couple will have to reject their old expectations and create new ones that are custom-made for their relationship.

For example, when Lyddy and Gary finally figured out what was happening, they were able to compromise in the following manner:

> **Lyddy:** "I will be responsible only for paying bills. I won't take complete responsibility for investments or major financial decisions."

> **Gary:** "I will be responsible only for seventy percent of our income."

> **They:** "We will choose our investments together."

Now they had each set limits they could live with. Both knew exactly what to do and what to expect from the other. Lyddy and Gary eliminated the role messages they had absorbed from their families and created new roles and expectations for each other.

People brought up in families with strict religious traditions may acquire different role messages they enact as adults. For instance, Carl grew up thinking "good Christian women" were quiet, demure, and submissive to their husbands. His wife, Haley, on the other hand, grew up in a Christian family where her mother was outspoken, fun-loving, and assertive.

You can imagine the disillusionment Carl and Haley experienced in their marriage. Consciously, they had assumed that the only really important thing was that they were both Christians. They had not realized that not all Christians had the same type of marriage.

It was impossible for Carl and Haley to reconcile their expectations of each other. They tried to set limits, but they just could not refrain from crossing each other's personal boundaries. They divorced after five years.

It is impossible to know everything about your partner when you commit to him or her. Setting personal boundaries takes a lifetime of discovering and renegotiating limits. A love relationship cannot be a power circle in motion if the partners are determined to resolve things only once for the rest of their lives.

People are not static. Even if you did know everything about your partner after two years, almost all of it would change after two more years. We change, we grow, we discover, we compromise, and hopefully we take the time to love and to enjoy. This is a vital part of living as two arcs joined in the power circle of partnership: be willing to let time pass.

Letting Time Pass

Part of the backlash of the obsession with dysfunction in the eighties was that many methods of recovery spent a lot of time dwelling on the past and on things that could not be changed. It is important to examine the past, digest its effects, and use what is learned in order to become the best person possible. However, recovery from a dysfunctional past becomes dysfunctional itself when individuals continue to dwell on—and even use—their tragedies as excuses not to make the most of the present.

Just as repeatedly picking a scab off a wound can delay healing, so picking at the past can hinder emotional growth. Sometimes it is necessary to uncover an old emotional wound in order to expose it for cleaning and treatment; this is perfectly healthy. But to keep scratching at inner wounds is not much different than unnecessarily causing an outer wound to bleed anew. Sometimes it is best to leave things alone and give them time to heal on their own accord.

Leaving dysfunction behind in any relationship is important. But you must take the first step and get busy. Start living and stop worrying about the little things. If you let time pass, your wounds may heal, and things will improve.

Kerry and Hal struggled greatly with this after Kerry had an affair. As they worked to save their relationship, they found it particularly hard to stop dwelling on Kerry's affair. Hal would typically make a comment that alluded to the affair; Kerry would be hurt and defensive; Hal would say something more overt; and then Kerry would blame him for not letting go of the past. A terrible argument usually would ensue, and the pain would only be reinforced.

Of course it is understandable why this type of problem is hard to leave behind. Affairs often break bonds of trust between people. Betrayal, insecurities, fears of abandonment, anger, guilt, shame, blame, and all sorts of other negative feelings surface quickly once an affair has been brought out into the open.

Nevertheless, it is important to remember that healthy relationships do not need to break up. Therefore, when either partner cheats on the other, it is safe to assume that there were serious troubles that were not taken care of. This does not justify the affair; it only emphasizes that it takes two people to form a healthy partnership. The partner having the affair can be reacting to the pain in the relationship.

This was the case with Kerry and Hal. They should have faced their problems before Kerry became involved with another man. But they faced their problems after the affair. They renegotiated their relationship in counseling. After several months, the therapist suggested that they allow themselves time for their new knowledge, wisdom, and understanding to process and work for them.

So Kerry and Hal made a pact: for three months they would pretend that the affair never happened and see if their lives were different at the end of that time. They would then reevaluate and go from there.

Even though Hal didn't feel much differently about Kerry at this juncture, he agreed to follow through with it. After the three months, Kerry and Hal reported some amazing results to their therapist . Even though nothing had changed tangibly in their lives, their daily interactions with each other had improved. They also eliminated some of their negative feelings by spending more quality time together.

For the first time, Hal felt he could forgive Kerry completely. He finally had hope of trusting her again. Kerry was much less defensive and was beginning to forgive herself and feel like an equal partner again in their relationship.

Letting time pass after foundational damage is the only way to heal relational wounds. While we go about the business of living, all that we've learned and experienced will largely process itself and enable us to heal inwardly. This may not have succeeded for Kerry and Hal if they hadn't had an underlying respect for each other. Respect is fundamental to any relationship. If partners do not respect each other, it will be impossible for them to form healthy power circles.

Gaining Respect

Respect is not something that merely happens—it is earned between people. In order to respect others, however, you must first respect yourself. Do you have to earn your own respect? Yes. Do you learn how to respect yourself from your parents, teachers, and other adults when you are a child? Yes. But earning self-respect as an adult sometimes means going back and untangling false images that you absorbed as a child.

For example, Kirsten is forty years old. She remembers being taught all kinds of things about respectability.

> "My parents impressed upon me that it was respectable to own a home, dress nicely, always be clean, pay your bills on time, and be polite. My teachers taught me that it was respectable to get good grades, be a good citizen, get along with others, and go to college.
>
> "I know there were many other things I picked up along the way from adults about being respectable, but these stick out in my mind—they are the roots of severe personal problems I've battled with in gaining my self-respect.
>
> "You see, after high school I did not attend college. I shared an apartment with some friends and went to work. I fell into the credit-card lifestyle very quickly and got in debt over my head. To top it off, one of my roommates took advantage of the fact that all the bills and the lease were in my name. She moved out after months of not paying her share, and I got stuck with all the bills. I had let it go so long because I'd

learned it was important to get along with people. I thought that meant not confronting them, even when I was being used.

"To make a long story short, I ended up filing for bankruptcy. So there I was in my mid-twenties—no home, bad credit, no college education, and bitterness about what getting along with others had cost me. I never consciously thought about those days again until I went into therapy ten years later with severe personal problems. It took me two years to untangle them. One of my core issues was that I had no respect for myself. The rules of my upbringing were so ingrained in me that I lost any respect I may have had by not living up to my preconceived definition of respectability.

"I literally had to strip away the layers of shame and guilt and start over. I redefined what was respectable and what was not. I had to separate material possessions from personal attributes. I learned that people who live in apartments are just as respectable as homeowners. I also learned that just because someone has a Ph.D. does not mean that he or she is necessarily a good or respectable person. I realized that sometimes things happen that are out of our control—maybe the bills can't always be paid on time or even paid at all. Most important, I learned that getting along with others meant asserting my own needs, even if it sometimes warranted their disapproval.

"I gained self-respect because I made my own rules and standards. I honor myself by living within my own code of conduct. Because I finally respect myself, I am now able to respect my partner, coworkers, and other people I care about."

Kirsten learned a valuable lesson: before you can respect others, especially those close to you, you must first respect yourself. Respecting your partner does not necessarily mean living by the exact same standards as he or she does. It means recognizing those differences in living habits or routines and *accepting* them and your partner as unique.

The following guidelines might help your relationship:

1. You must have your own inner code of ethics.

2. You must live by this code to respect yourself.

3. You must honor your partner's code of ethics.

4. You must accept that his or her code will be somewhat different from yours.

5. You must be prepared to end the relationship if your values are so different that it is impossible to hold each other in high esteem.

If your partnership is to last, it must include mutual respect. Otherwise, the ups and downs of life will slowly wear on your relationship until there is absolutely *no* respect left, and the relationship dies. If, however, you find that this section of the book has given you a greater understanding of yourself and your partner, then you are more likely to enjoy the longevity of a successful companionship.

To review briefly what we have discussed in the last three chapters, you and your loved one should . . .

○ Consider each other mutual partners.
○ Commit to each other.
○ Meet your own individual emotional needs.
○ Become more resilient.
○ Deal with the negative issues in your relationship.
○ Practice your renegotiating skills.
○ Set limits and follow through with them.
○ Let time pass and give love a chance.
○ Behave respectfully toward each other.

Loving for the Long Haul

Life is full of highs and lows. There are times of great joy and success. There are periods of stress and despair. But if you look at a roller coaster, you notice that much of the ride is spent pulling uphill or coasting downhill. Successful relationships commit to the ride and roll with the loops, hills, twists, turns, and valleys that life offers. It is not a good idea to jump into a serious relationship at the top of a hill; it is also unwise to bail out when the relationship's in a valley. We need to look at the big picture of our lives. We should make important decisions only during uphill climbs or downward coasts.

I hope that as you read over the following "Suggestions for Circling with Your Partner" you will gain further insights into making your love relationship stronger. I hope that yours is a true power circle and that your love will last over the long haul.

Suggestions for Circling with Your Partner

Have you ever gotten into an argument with your partner and in the middle of it had a moment of intense regret because you realize you are arguing about something other than the obvious issue? Perhaps your feelings were hurt because your partner was late for dinner—instead of sharing those feelings, you battle about who was supposed to wash the car. After the realization hits, you want to take back your angry words and stop fighting.

There are several things you can do if you find this happening when you argue. The most important thing, however, is to realize you are displacing your anger and to change the nature of the argument. You may want to try using humor: reach out and grab your mate's cheeks, give him or her a huge bear hug, or make a funny face. Excuse yourself, go to the bathroom, and paint a clown's smile on your mouth with lipstick. The more outrageous, the more fight-busting power the act will have.

If humor isn't your style, you may want to try using honesty. Simply tell your partner the truth about why you are upset. If he or she really loves you, your feelings will be well received and your honesty will be admired.

Another suggestion you may want to try for circling with your partner is to celebrate and renew your courting days or anniversary dates. Try planting a tree, shrub, or flower to remind you of the growing, changing process that all successful relationships go through. If you live in an apartment or do not have room to do this on your property, do your planting at a relative's or a friend's house.

At the time of planting, implement a ceremonial tradition of some sort that's personal to your relationship. Toast each other with champagne or cider. Reread your wedding vows, recite a poem, play a favorite song on a portable player, or say a prayer for each other. Whatever you do, your relationship will be strengthened as you reminisce about your early years together and fall in love with each other all over again.

Part III

Kids—The Insulated Circles

This

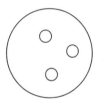

Not this

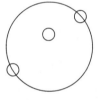

Chapter Seven
Spinning the Cocoon

I doubt there is a more soothing picture than that of two parents smiling warmly over their newborn baby. As a society, we want desperately to think that the world is safe and family-friendly. Television commercials and programs repeatedly tug at our heartstrings with glowing images from the bygone days of imagined family unity and consistency.

Nostalgia has its place, but in order to remain functioning in today's world, we need to accept that these hallowed days of memories are gone—if they ever really existed. There can be no going back. However, we can take the best from those years and the best of what we now know, weave these healthy memories together, and spin cocoons of love, warmth, and strength around our children.

Simultaneously we can be savvy and safe; sophisticated and fun-loving; realistic and hope-filled; healthy and happy. In fact, if we think back and are truly honest, there were a lot of things we would *not* want to relive from our pasts—children being shuffled around by mothers, paddled with wooden spoons by fathers, and encouraged to be "seen and not heard." It was not at all rare for family members to know one another only slightly. In fact, many families did not have what we strive for so diligently today: real relationships.

There is a reason why we suffer today and why many of us long for healthy, fulfilled lives. We know there were things that did not work from observing past generations. We are breaking new ground, but we are not armed with all of the information or experience we need to keep things in balance.

However, we have learned much. And together, we can continue to learn. We can become better people and improve our relationships by sharing what we know with various sources: 1) personal networks, 2) doctors and therapists, 3) pastors and teachers, 4) judicial systems, and 5) the public, through writing books like this. The more we learn, share, and refine, the better equipped we are to lead healthy lives as round circles that insulate our children.

One thing any parent will agree with is that adding children to a relationship, whether in a nuclear, nontraditional, or blended household, is a very challenging proposition.

Mixing Partnerships with Children

Even if our own inner circle is in good shape and our partnership is in power circle mode, mixing children into the formula will add many complicated dimensions to life. For each child, there are relationship considerations in multiples of the number of people already in the family. I call this the family formula multiple.

For example, one child plus two parents equals three persons. There will be three times the considerations because the child has relationships with his or her "self" and with two parents. Reciprocally, each parent has a relationship with self, the other parent, and the child. This is actually the simplest of family formula multiples, with a factor of three times three resulting in nine various relationships in the family.

An average nuclear family—with two parents and two children—has a family formula multiple of sixteen. In practice, the family formula multiple looks something like this:

> Janie is twelve. One night she comes out of her room dressed for a school dance. Dad explodes because he thinks Janie's clothes and makeup are too seductive. Mom is ambivalent. She agrees with Dad but sympathizes with Janie. Janie's

brother, Josh, is fourteen. He says sarcastically that Janie looks like a "geek" to him. Mom chastises Josh. Dad reiterates his disapproval of Janie's attire. Janie bursts into tears. Josh rolls his eyes and begins to laugh. The entire family of four is now in an uproar. But we must multiply this times four because each member of the family is experiencing different feelings toward the situation and towards each other. Dad is reacting to his fear of his daughter growing up. Mom is remembering when her father was too strict with her. Janie is thinking ahead to what her peers will think if she cannot dress like the rest of the sixth graders. And Josh is looking out for his peer position too—he doesn't want his friends to ridicule him because his sister looks like a "geek." A situation between two family members has now involved all four members and their relationships to each other.

Think about many of our blended families today: two children, two parents, two stepchildren, two ex-partners, and often, two new partners. We now have a family formula multiple of ONE HUNDRED! This means that for every family interaction there is a potential combination of one hundred subtle or overt reactions that may take place among family members.

No wonder mixing partnerships with children is challenging! Whether yours is a nuclear, nontraditional, or blended family, you will face the family formula multiple the day a child comes into your life. This is a fact of family life. It is in your entire family's best interest to accept this, make the best of it, and consider it when you feel as though you are not going to make it.

Fighting against this truth will only add frustration, discontentment, and disappointment to your life. In fact, trying to force your family into clean, uncomplicated relationships is a no-win situation. It is impossible for human beings, with all of their idiosyncrasies and individual needs, to relate in simplistic ways all of the time.

One of the problems from past generations was the great effort by families to appear to be "perfect" to those outside of their immediate family. These families often ignored their family formula multiples, as well as the needs of individual family members. If a daughter got pregnant in one of these families, she was often sent away to save the family from embarrassment. If a son was arrested for driving under the influence of alcohol, he would bring shame to the whole family.

Of course, this still happens today, but we are learning. More and more we begin to understand that our children are separate people who make their own decisions. We know in our heads that we cannot completely control our children, that no one is perfect, that impressions can be largely deceiving, and that the choices our children make are not necessarily reflections of the choices we would make for ourselves or them.

But our hearts do not always go along with what our heads know to be true. When children come into our lives, we desperately want them to grow up in a safe, loving, and carefree environment. Often, we subconsciously promise our children things we can't deliver: we will keep them from pain; we will give them all the material perks of a good life; we will protect them from heartbreaks and failures; and we will generally keep them away from every cruel reality.

Yes, each child should be in her or his own circle, insulated within the power circle of a healthy partnership. But this does not mean that children are immune to (or should be protected from) reality. It means that we should protect them in appropriate ways until they are prepared to emerge from the power circle as mature individuals in circle shapes of their own.

If this is the end goal, then we can see how imperative it is to be aware of and accept the reality of the family formula multiple and to let go of the unrealistic commitments we make to our children to keep them from the normal pains and suffering of life.

Unwritten Rules, Unspoken Vows

As we parent our children, all kinds of inner "deals" (made with ourselves) surface that we never knew existed. One mother I know grew up in poverty and was taunted for not having nice clothes, a car, or money to go to cheerleading camp. She vowed that her children would never, never be poor. Unfortunately, she and her husband have had tremendous financial difficulties and struggled with poverty for years. It took an emotional breakdown and several months of therapy before this woman consciously realized that her financial problems were not the only stresses that contributed to her breakdown. The vows she made to her children (which were impossible and unnecessary to fulfill) were also contributors. She wanted to "save" her children from poverty for two reasons: 1) so they would not have to suffer the same indignities that she had endured, and 2) so *she* would not have to suffer through them further.

A father I spoke with was so determined that his children did not experience the same pain he had faced as a teenager with severe acne, crooked teeth, and a birthmark on his neck that he spent thousands of dollars on orthodontists, dermatologists, cosmeticians, and even a plastic surgeon to make his kids blemish-free.

The problem was that his children did not live by the same, subconscious agenda their father did. They simply grew up thinking appearances were everything. Now they are spoiled, shallow young adults who constantly pelt their father with requests for money to indulge their own vanity.

Tony is another example of a child who was negatively affected by his father's parental vows: he nearly lost his life because of them. Tony's father was obese as a child. As a result, other kids were cruel to him, his activities were restricted, his health was negatively impacted, and his self-esteem was low. He determined that "no son of mine would ever live with this problem."

Tony's childhood was riddled with dietary restrictions. He couldn't eat sweets. He always had to eat on schedule. He even had to bring his own sack lunches when he visited other children's homes. His father enforced this diet until Tony was substantially deprived and resented his father. In addition, Tony was required to keep up a physical fitness regimen that many adults would be unable to perform. His father had him doing calisthenics, weightlifting, and aerobic training morning and night, seven days a week, with hardly any rest.

Tony made a vow to himself that when he escaped his father's tyranny he would never discipline himself with diet or fitness. True to his vow, Tony indulged himself decadently as a young adult. He ate and ate and ate. He consumed far too much alcohol and experimented with other drugs. He didn't do so much as one sit-up while he was in college.

Ironically, the more out of shape and heavier Tony became, the more his father's parenting messages haunted him. Tony finally gave in to his childhood programming. He returned to his father's regime and stuck to it. Only this time he became such a health fanatic that he went to the other end of the spectrum and became bulimic. In his early thirties, the electrolyte balance in Tony's body went askew, and he nearly died of a heart attack. He's been in and out of therapy for years, trying to achieve and maintain a more balanced diet and lifestyle for himself.

Although extreme, Tony's story does bear out the truth of how very important it is that we, as parents, make conscious commitments to seek out our own unspoken vows and unwritten rules. We need to bring these to light and cope with them ourselves—not impose them upon our children!

Through better understanding of how the family formula multiple and your own unspoken vows can affect your family's life, you can consciously begin to make choices to ensure that your kids are truly insulated circles within the power circle of a healthy relationship.

Changing Your "Dreamscape"

As stated earlier, the challenges of mixing partnerships with children are complicated by the family formula multiple. They are further burdened by the unspoken vows and unwritten rules that we have regarding our children. Another element that can add to the complexity of parenting are the hopes and dreams we create for our kids. These may be dreams we had for ourselves and did not fulfill; dreams our parents had for us that we rejected; dreams we feel will be flattering to us; or dreams society has deemed as "good" for our kids to pursue.

Notice that none of these reasons derive solely from the hope that our children may fulfill their *own* dreams for their *own* reasons, at their *own* pace, and in their *own* ways. They are for us; a part of each reason is for our own or other people's satisfaction.

Notice, also, that many "good" dreams involve financial success. Society has become so entrenched in money, material wealth, corporate power, and glamour that we have lost touch with the reality that people can be happy, fulfilled, and successful without any of those things!

Stop looking to the media and other outside sources for definitions of what is good, bad, successful, or failing. Quit looking at fashion models and posters to tell you what "perfect" bodies should look like. Halt your incessant search for the "magic key" to happiness and well-being.

To become healthy adults, we need to change our "dreamscapes." Our kids must be valued and honored for simply existing—not for how high their grades are, what awards they get in athletics, who their friends are, or how well they conform to our image of "good." The dreams we help plant in our children's precious little hearts need to come from who they naturally are.

In the first section of this book, I talked about making commitments to contend for our own niches in life. If our children are to be healthy, insulated circles in our care, then we need to give up our dreams for them and let them find their own. We need to start over and nurture our kids so they can become the people they were born to be, not the ones that we think they *should* be.

How do we, as parents, form new "dreamscapes" and allow our children to search for their own? Here are a few tips:

1. Find some quiet time to sit down with a pencil and paper. Relax. Allow yourself to daydream about your life as you envisioned it before you had any children.

2. Write a list of the dreams you recall. Did you want to be a ballerina? Did you see yourself as an oil magnate? A professional tennis player? A rock star? What did you want to be when you grew up?

3. Now list the aspirations you knew (or sensed) your parents had for you. Did they want you to become a doctor? A lawyer? An astronaut? A politician? The heir to the family business?

4. Next, list each of your children separately and the careers or lifestyles you think would be good for each of them to pursue. Do you have a fashion model in the family? A navy captain? A professional race car driver? A marine biologist?

5. Look for parallels. Do you want your children to achieve what you yourself did not? Are there similarities in your hopes for your kids to those your parents had for you? Have you bought society's bill of goods that only the thin, attractive, rich, and famous are really successful? Truly look at the lists. Are you allowing your kids to become what is most natural and best for them? Or are you forcing dance, piano, golf, and other types of training on your kids, trying to make them turn out the way you hope?

6. Finally, vow that you will make every effort possible to observe each of your children or stepchildren in their daily lives. Choose, through silent observation and unmanipulative questions, to help them seek out what is in their hearts. According to your means, provide activities, lessons, exposure, and other opportunities for each child to try his or her hand at different things they seem to have a predisposition for or curiosity about.

For example, a daughter who loves horses could work at a local ranch or stable after school. Another child who has a propensity for art can take lessons, visit museums and galleries, or be given art supplies as a birthday present. A son may want to spend his time baking. You can order brochures from culinary schools for him to look over, ask him to try new recipes for you, and order him a subscription for a gourmet food magazine. There are dozens of other ways for you to change your "dreamscape" for your children and to encourage them to create their own.

This may be time-consuming, messy, inconvenient, and even a hardship at times. But isn't it worth it? What better insulation can you give your priceless "circles" than the means to find their own dreams? After all, we give our children life, but only they can choose how they will live. Once we have our young reared, it is our responsibility to let them go.

Giving Them Life to Let Them Live

Sally and Lester had done a commendable job with their brood of eight children. Sally was a homemaker until her youngest child was in junior high school. Then she completed paralegal training and went to work. Lester will retire next year after working forty-five years for the same utility company. Each of their children has chosen a different career direction. All but two say they are completely satisfied. Here are some of their children's comments about their choices and how their parents contributed to their success in pursuing and finding their own dreams:

Norris is forty-four. He owns and operates an animal petting farm with his wife and children about an hour away from a large city.

> He says, "We've never been rich and probably never will be, but I wouldn't trade the family lifestyle, being outdoors, working with animals, and meeting all kinds of people for anything! I think Mom and Dad played an important part in my finding my place in life by always praising my ideas and dreams as a kid. No matter what crazy scheme I came up with, they said it was great, and they knew I could accomplish anything I wanted. Well, this is what I wanted, and it is what I have."

Holly is forty-two. She is the mayor of a small California city.

> She notes, "My parents taught me that it didn't matter what sex, race, or religion a person is. They told us we could break through any barriers just by being true to ourselves and our abilities. But my husband could not abide by that. He wanted a little woman at home to bear children, cook, and clean. Even though my mother did this full-time for many years, she never once made me feel that it was my only option. I think my husband thought he was marrying my mother. In many ways he did, just not the at-home version. We divorced five years ago."

Andrew is thirty-nine. He owns a small family resort on a lake in Minnesota, and his wife is an architect. They have two small children who stay with Andrew during the day and help him run the resort.

Andrew says, "I think the best thing my parents passed on to me was showing me how to respect a mate. My wife often says that she is grateful to my dad for teaching me how to be a husband who values his wife. My parents demonstrated such equal consideration and high regard for each other and us kids that I wouldn't think of treating my wife, my kids, or myself in any other way."

Candace is thirty-seven. She is a teacher and one of the two grown children who is discontented with her life.

She says, "I think I fell in love with the *idea* of being a teacher—not the reality of the profession. I am presently brainstorming ways to use my education and qualifications in a different field. I know that I will do this and succeed, largely because my parents instilled in us that our life is our own responsibility and that if we choose to be miserable, then we choose to betray ourselves.

"In fact, when I told my parents I felt guilty about wanting to leave teaching because they helped put me through college, Daddy said, 'That may well be, but that was so you could help yourself to be happy in whatever you chose to do. I don't recall you being born with teacher tattooed on your butt.' I guess with that kind of common sense and support behind me, I can't lose."

Ellen is thirty-six. She and her husband are foster parents. They have had up to six youngsters in their home at one time. Ellen says her parents babysit one night a month so she and her husband can get out without worrying.

"My parents are very giving people, but they are also very assertive. If we tried to take advantage of their kindness and asked them repeatedly to babysit, they would have no problems refusing and would feel just fine with it. I think they taught me that being assertive is in everyone's best interest.

"I am comfortable with who I am because my parents made me feel loved and wanted. This love is what enables me to take children from troubled homes and plant seeds of hope in their lives. I am fulfilling their needs, as well as my own. I think when parents give up who they are 'for the sake of the kids,' they leave incredible shame and guilt in the wake.

"I never doubted my parents' loyalty to us and to each other. They had the perfect balance: they were committed to the family and committed to their own individuality at the same time. It gave me a solid foundation on which to build my own happy marriage."

Patsy is thirty-three. She is the pastor of a large Protestant church. She speaks of her mother and father as being first and foremost "human."

"My parents never played games with us kids. They didn't try to pretend they were perfect or try to play God with us. When they made mistakes, they admitted them. And they enjoyed their successes completely. They didn't let others step all over them, but they weren't afraid to give of themselves either. I guess a healthy balance is what they passed on to me. With the self-confidence and leadership skills they gave me, I felt that pastoring others—many of whom were much less fortunate in their families of origin—helped me perpetuate my parents' wisdom to others."

Renee is thirty-one. She is the administrator of a nursing home.

She notes, "Many people come to this care facility to die. The most heartbreaking situations are those in which the residents are alone. Maybe there are a few courtesy visits by grown children or grandchildren, but basically they are deserted. I always wonder what kind of family life there was when the children don't have enough regard for their aging and dying parents to make sure they are a part of their lives.

"My parents loved us with such unconditional love and respect that I can't imagine not visiting them as often as I could if they were in a nursing home. I can't conceive of not helping them make the transitions involved or not being a regular presence in their lives. I guess my parents cared enough about us kids to let us go. In this way, they gave us the freedom to always go back to them, too."

Mark is twenty-eight. He says he unwittingly participated in fulfilling the dream a high school guidance counselor recommended to him.

"This guy told me that biochemistry was the rage of the future. He shoved literature, schools, money, and all the perks down my throat until I swallowed it. Now I'm a biochemist all right. The guidance counselor may be happy, but I'm sure not. I keep remembering my mother saying, 'Don't ever try to live out the dreams of others because you'll only end up with nightmares.' Now I know what she meant.

"It will take a while, but I am going back to school and using my education to become a doctor, which is what I always wanted to be anyway. I can't believe I let a guy who barely knew me steer me in the wrong direction. But then thank God for my parents. They never pressured us to stick with anything just because we decided to do it. In fact, Dad always said if we were doing something we didn't like we'd better have a pretty darn good reason for wasting ourselves. Since they gave me the choice to be happy, I'm also free to forgive myself for my mistakes and turn them into building blocks for better things."

I doubt there is a parent anywhere who wouldn't love to have their children say similar things about them. Sally and Lester have done a superb job in raising eight wonderful kids. However, they have also had their share of ups and downs and were not immune to the pain and suffering of live.

For instance, Patsy had two abortions in her early college days. Ellen was addicted to drugs throughout high school. Norris was in jail for draft dodging in the late 1960s. Holly's divorce left her depressed and suicidal for two years—she lived with Sally and Lester much of that time. Renee was recently diagnosed with multiple sclerosis. And Mark had an affair with the wife of one of his professors and caused a campus-wide scandal.

Many of the grandchildren, of all ages, have received various life "bruises" as well. One has Down's syndrome, one is pregnant, and another has AIDS. There is hardly a time when someone in this large, extended family isn't hurting or in some kind of trouble.

> When asked if it was all worth it, Lester says immediately, "Of course, it's all worth it—if you're not prepared to allow your kids to live, then you shouldn't give them life at all!"

Sally and Lester had a family formula multiple of one hundred in their nuclear family alone. Now, counting in-laws, grandchildren, their spouses, and children (a total of thirty-six), the multiple has grown to 1,296! Thankfully, not everyone lives in the same town or interacts on a personal level every day. Still, they *are* all interconnected and that seems extremely overwhelming. How can they be part of such a large network and still remain in circle balance with themselves, with their relationships, and with their children?

The answer is to live by this vital truth: *you only control yourself and your own reactions*. In fact, the only healthy way to deal with the family formula multiple is to etch this truth deeply into your psyche and lifestyle. When you live by it, your unwritten rules, unspoken vows, and "dreamscapes" become unnecessary. And your whole life takes on a circling motion that is healthy and free of dysfunction.

In the next chapter we will discuss more specifics about "Kids—The Insulated Circles." We will explore discipline, relationship triangles, adolescent problems, consequences, and healthy ways of parenting from a distance.

But first you may find the following exercise valuable in practicing the philosophy, "I only control me and my reactions."

Exercise: I Only Control Me and My Reactions!

Play out the following scenarios in your mind. Then act them out in your family or discuss them as a group.

Scenario 1
Upon rising one morning, you go to the kitchen and put on a pot of coffee. You hear someone stirring in the living room. It is your sixteen-year-old son and his girlfriend entangled in blankets, still fast asleep. They have obviously spent the night there together.

Scenario 2
Your thirteen-year-old daughter comes home from a movie and goes right to bed. A short while later, as you pass by her door, you hear her vomiting. You rush into her room to find her throwing up in her waste basket. The smell of peppermint liqueur is lingering in the air.

Scenario 3
Your seventeen-year-old has always wanted to go to college and has worked to achieve this goal ever since first grade. In her junior year of high school, however, she decides she doesn't care about college anymore. Her grades drop, she starts skipping school, and she quits the basketball team.

Scenario 4
Your fifteen-year-old son insists on dating a nineteen-year-old girl. Even though you have repeatedly forbade him to go out with her, you catch him sneaking out his window one night as he says there is nothing you can do to stop him from seeing her.

Think these scenarios through carefully. Consider how little control you actually have over the choices and behaviors of others—including your children. Each person has the power and ability to make his or her own decisions about how to think, act, and feel. It is healthy to repeat to yourself, whenever you can, "I only control me and my reactions."

Chapter Eight
0 to 18 in 6,570 Days

Nearly every parent has received advice from other parents of older or grown children that sounds something like this, "Enjoy your kids while they're little—time goes so fast that before you know it, they'll be grown and gone, and you'll miss them terribly." When we hear this advice, we tend to look at our toddler—as he or she pulls something off a counter or dumps something onto the floor—and say, "I don't think so."

But the truth is that most of us find the advice is very accurate. Time does pass quickly. Our children do grow up and go their separate ways— often before we are prepared to let them go. However, when our children are preschoolers, and we find ourselves overwhelmed by the tremendous adjustments in our lives, we may wonder if they'll ever be more tractable and less demanding. In ways, yes. But in many other ways, NO! Once we have these tiny babes in our arms we have begun a journey that will forever change us—and will probably, at times, extract great tolls from our hearts.

The journey from age 0 to age 18 is 6,570 days long. This by no means indicates that your job as a parent will be over when your child is eighteen. It is simply a fact that may put things into perspective. When you are pacing the floor trying to pacify a four-month-old, colicky baby, you may want to remember that you only have about 6,450 days left to go. When that baby is up during the night with pangs of teething at eight months, you can count down another 120 days.

When this baby is three years old, lying in the middle of the grocery store aisle throwing a tantrum, you can be assured that the next 5,475 days *will* pass. As you send your new kindergartner off to school at age five—feeling as if your heart may break with pain and burst with pride at the same time—you have less than 5,000 days to go. When that kindergartner is a little league pitcher and gets knocked flat by a ball when he or she is eight, and it seems an eternity before you can get to him or her, bear up—it's only another 3,650 days until graduation!

By the time your child is nearing the threshold of adolescence, at twelve years old or so, and begins to experience the moods of awakening hormones, hold on—you're only about 2,200 days away from eighteen. When you have a full-blown case of "teenager" on your hands, at age sixteen, and think you'll never make it through driving, dating, and God only knows what else, hang tight—only about 700 days to go.

Finally, when your "baby" reaches his or her eighteenth birthday and you feel the sands of life shifting under your feet, you may want to know you've given him or her everything necessary to function in an extremely complex world. Now it is too late to turn the calendar back. Time has passed. Whether you like it or not, your influence as a parent will begin to wane from this day on. So, whether you are expecting your first child or getting ready to allow your fourth to leave the nest, you have (or have had) the same number of days between birth and age eighteen.

Back to Basics—Discipline!

Several years ago, a psychologist I know named Frank and his wife, Debbie, were having a very difficult time parenting their daughter. (I think many of us can appreciate their dilemma.) Just like many others who are now forty-something, Frank and Debbie entered parenthood thinking it was better to talk with their children than it was to spank or punish them. When Andrea was born, they made a vow to raise her with patience and loving guidance rather than with any physical punishment.

When I first met them, Andrea was seven years old. I was a little uncomfortable around them and usually remained silent when the subject of discipline came up—their discussions were filled with what I felt was a lot of psycho-babble; it reflected little hands-on reality. My own boys were Andrea's age and younger, but I had found that without firm guidelines, my boys went out of control. Rhetoric is fine for philosophical discussions, but kids need to know that their parents are confidently in charge of the family.

One day, Frank and Debbie joined me for lunch. I immediately knew something serious was troubling them. When I asked what it was, their parenting problems poured out. It seemed that their vow to talk Andrea through childhood was burdening their lives to the extent that they could hardly stand being around her, and, as a result, they were experiencing severe marital stress. Their extended family and other friends were on edge for entire visits because Andrea was so demanding and disruptive.

> Frank ended by asking me in complete exasperation, "What do you think?!!"

> I considered backing away and remaining noncommittal in my stance but decided that honesty would best serve the situation. I said, "I think it sounds like Andrea is a spoiled rotten brat and that you two need to act like adults and take control of your family!"

Frank and Debbie looked at me in genuine perplexity. I could see they had no idea what I meant—they thought they *were* in control. I realized I had a lot of explaining to do:

> "Look, guys, let me give you a few examples of what I mean. First, I've heard you both talk about not being able to go to sleep because Andrea isn't ready to go to sleep. You've also complained about Andrea being crabby because she didn't want to take a nap. I think that's downright baloney! She's the child; you're the adults. She should go to bed when you want her to.

> "Second, I've heard you tell stories of her 'making you' get her treats and other things in stores. She can't make you do anything. You allow her to boss you around. You also say how

frustrated you get when she won't pick up her toys or do other things you tell her to do. Well, you make the rules, and it's up to you to enforce them. It seems to me that Andrea does not have any consequences for misbehavior or poor choices.

"I'm not saying you need to be punitive, but she needs to have very clear boundaries drawn when it comes to how much power you give her. Kids will take power, but that doesn't mean they prefer it or are comfortable with it. You've let Andrea break whatever boundaries you may have previously set for her. She's been getting her way for so long, you will have to be very firm with her until she gets used to your new way of handling things."

As I spoke, I could see Frank and Debbie's eyes begin to open and expand. It had never occurred to them that they were doing Andrea a great disservice by not disciplining her. After talking a while longer, they agreed that they needed to change their disciplinary action—or create one, for that matter.

Together, we came up with a back-to-basics discipline and philosophy plan to help them control Andrea. (This plan may be helpful for you, also.)

1. Parents Head the Family

Children need to know that a parent or other adult is the boss! They gain great comfort and security in knowing that their parent is in control of the household. This frees children to be kids—to explore, to experiment, to test rules, and to begin learning who they are. You may never win any popularity contests this way, but parenting isn't a contest; it is a solemn responsibility. Children should be given power only in age-appropriate increments.

For example, a ten-year-old still needs a definite bedtime; a good night's sleep is much more important than watching television. Although you decide when bedtime is, you should also give the child some power. Let him or her choose parts of the schedule, but only within your parameters. He or she can decide when to bathe, do homework, and relax, but you decide when he or she goes to bed and eats dinner. This will help the child develop self-discipline while also learning to respect your authority and to trust you more.

2. Parents Make the Rules

Again, do not do your children damage by overloading them with too much power. You may allow them to make their own rules within your rules or let them choose among options you give them, but don't burden them with major decisions. Sometimes they need you to take stands they aren't ready to take. For example, a twelve-year-old daughter may beg to go to the movies with a boy, but inside she is feeling nervous about actually going. She may need you to set the limit for her by saying "No." When you do say, "No," she may go off in a huff, but she is probably relieved she doesn't have to go.

Parenthood is full of paradoxes like this. That is why it is important for us to do what we know is right or what our instincts tell us is good. We should not make our decisions based on our children's actions. Of course, we must also take time to examine our rules periodically. We must review their validity and make sure our reasons for having them are truly in the best interest of our children.

3. Parents Enforce the Rules

Rules are only as good as their enforcement. If your children know that you say what you mean and mean what you say, they will have respect for you both as a person and as a parent. Integrity, consistency, and fairness are vital ingredients to enforcing rules. If you tell your child that bedtime is nine o'clock and continuously vary this, the child will start doubting your word. If you allow a youngster to talk back to you one time, and another time you punish the child for the same infraction, she or he will begin to mistrust you and look for ways to lessen interaction with you. However, if you are often too harsh in enforcing rules, your child will avoid having a genuine relationship with you.

Children are very good at reading situations and manipulating them for their own gain. Even a five-year-old child knows that if one parent says "No," there is a possibility that the other will say, "Yes." The child will likely go for the opening. If both parents disagree and argue about it, the child will feel a surge of power and remember the method for future use. Again, you must enforce the rules with integrity, consistency, and fairness. This will provide a sturdy foundation for your family that will carry you through the teen years.

4. Set Boundaries Among Family Members

Discipline is intimately related to respect. Therefore, it is imperative that you respect yourself, your partner, and each of your children—and that they respect you. A good example of this is privacy. Family members should know the rules specific to your household. Perhaps it is not acceptable to barge into the bathroom without knocking or to take belongings of other family members without asking. Boundaries can be created by you and your children in a myriad of ways. You may teach a child not to take food from other people's plates during meals, not to come into your bedroom if the door is closed, not to interrupt a conversation, or not to open other people's mail.

Be aware that whatever types of boundaries you set for yourself will likely be the kind your children learn to set for themselves. If you have a difficult time setting limits with your time, energy, love, and money, your children will also when they are adults. Be conscientious about the examples and rules you set.

5. Let Consequences Be Natural

When enforcing rules and drawing boundaries, let the consequences of your child's choices and behaviors be as natural as possible. If he or she breaks the homework rule at your house and doesn't get a paper done, let the child get a zero—do not stay up until midnight doing the work yourself! If your child has made a commitment to save up the money to buy a guitar and doesn't meet the goal, don't you buy it! Rescuing children only keeps them dependent on you.

One of the things my parents used to do when my siblings and I were arguing was to make us each sit on separate chairs in the same room. They told us we had to stay put until we worked out our differences. The first ten minutes were usually spent making faces at each other and calling each other names.

One of us would usually sneak in a "Can we get up now?"

My mother would respond from another room, "Not until you can get along."

We'd sit there a few more minutes sticking out our tongues at one another until one of us would figure out that we were only hurting ourselves—our parents really meant what they said. Someone would reluctantly make a peace offering. It was usually rejected the first time, but eventually we came around and were allowed to go happily on our way. Notice I didn't say we had to agree with one another or give in to one another—we had to work out our differences on our own. Now I see the long-term wisdom of this. I don't think it is a coincidence that I get along quite well with many different types of people. I always work through my differences with people, so we can go on living without holding grudges.

If my parents had isolated us from each other or scolded us for arguing, we might very well have learned to run away from our problems rather than work them out. Natural consequences are much, much more effective than arbitrary punishments. If you spank a child for spilling milk, he or she will simply think you're mean. However, if you make your child clean up the mess and supervise calmly, he or she will soon take responsibility for any actions—accident or not. The best kind of discipline is to allow your children to experience the natural consequences of their choices and behaviors.

6. Discipline Should Teach Children How to Take Care of Themselves

Every once in a while you should evaluate your discipline plan. If you are satisfied that you are clearly the head of your family—you make the rules, you enforce the rules, you teach healthy boundaries, and you allow your children's consequences to be as natural as possible—you may want to take mental inventory. Ask yourself, "Are my children learning things that will help them take care of themselves when they are adults?" If the answer is, "Yes," then you're most likely on the right track. I'm not talking about forcing little ones to behave like miniature adults. I am referring to age-appropriate responsibilities you can give them to help them in their future.

For instance, does your eleven-year-old keep her clothes folded and put away? Or are you constantly following behind her picking them up? Stop it! If she's happy in wrinkled clothes let her be. Someday she'll probably decide she wants to be neater and start taking better care of her clothes. Does your seven-year-old hate it when her preschool-aged brother plays with the toys that she left out? Don't put them away! She can do this for herself if she really doesn't want the younger one to touch them.

Back-to-basic discipline merely means using your common sense. Keep your kids safe. Be the grown-up. Don't neglect your children. Let them do for themselves what they can and teach them the rest. The whole family will be happier and healthier because of the maturity, love, and guidance you've given them. It takes time, effort, and a great deal of energy to be a good parent. But don't ever underestimate the return on your investment. It is the best feeling in the world when your grown child tells you that you did a great job and that he or she is glad to be your kid!

Frank and Debbie soon realized how lenient they had been with Andrea. They now knew what they had to do to raise a controllable, responsible daughter. Before they left, I reiterated the necessity for firm guidance. I told them the entire family benefits when the parents are in a healthy power circle, and the children are given the security of their insulation.

When parents do not take responsibility, neglect their children, or give them too much power, the children become oval-shaped eggs, clinging and linked to the parents' circles. Too much weight is burdened on the relationships within the family, and codependency often results. Many times, the parents also find themselves pulling on each other. Dangerous triangles can result among parents and children; triangles simply do not work in relationships!

Triangles—The Shapes That Don't Work

Frank and Debbie had allowed Andrea to be the third point of a triangle. Andrea would typically ask Frank for something; if he responded in a way she did not like, she would overtly approach Debbie. If Debbie did not back Frank up, Andrea was off and running. Even at seven years old, she was very adept at causing problems between her parents. She knew what issues were sensitive, and she seemed to revel in the power she had to stir up trouble. Frank and Debbie fell for Andrea's tricks nearly every time. They deluded themselves into thinking they simply disagreed with each other—they thought it was better to be honest with Andrea rather than give in to the other to provide a united front for Andrea. Each parent would rather have the other angry with him or her than with Andrea.

What a delicate issue! It is so important for caregivers to present a united front. Again, during the volatile teen years, kids need to have a firm foundation already built by their parents. They need to see their parents as one powerful circle—not as two squabbling ovals. I do not mean that as parents you should allow each other to be abusive or negligent; it is imperative that your children be protected from these hostilities if they are to live a healthy adult life. What I do mean is that sometimes you may have to disagree with the other parent in order to protect your child. It's up to you to decide when to agree and when to disagree in front of your child. This can often be a very fine line to define.

For example, in our family, my husband does a lot more teasing than I would prefer. We strongly disagree, at times, on what is funny and what is ridiculing. Funny is okay; ridiculing is abusive. Over the years, we have had several arguments about the issue. When I felt that something was genuinely cruel, I said so. When he sincerely meant only to tease, he made this clear. But as much as possible, we present ourselves as being in agreement with—or at least supportive of—each other. Between us, I believe our boys got a well-rounded picture of the difference between teasing and ridiculing.

A common complaint from couples in a traditional nuclear family is that one parent is too strict, and the other is too soft. Sometimes this is related to gender. There seems to be a clear pattern of the way men and women handle their kids. Deborah Tannen, Ph.D., noted in her book *You Just Don't Understand* that women generally try to connect more closely with others, while men tend to rank people's status as either being "above" or "below" theirs (with an obvious preference to be above others). Women, she also notes, seek intimacy, while men seek independence.

This helps to explain why women and men communicate differently and why they have trouble interpreting the behaviors of the opposite sex. It does not mean that one way is right and the other wrong. It means that our children have the natural need and ability to adapt to some of both. It is our job, as parents, to find satisfactory ways of combining our differences for the benefit of our kids. Sometimes this is all but impossible. There will be situations when one parent feels so strongly about something that he or she follows through on his or her own decision, regardless of what the other parent thinks.

One mother, Nancy, felt it was absolutely imperative for her daughter, Emma, to have braces. The father, Vern, had grown up in poverty—orthodontics would never have been a remote consideration in his day. He thought braces were a ridiculous luxury, and he refused to pay for them. Nancy quietly told Vern this was very important to her, and she would see to it that Emma had braces. If Vern refused to pay for them, then she would. He was outraged.

Nancy explained to Emma that she was going directly against Vern's wishes and that ordinarily, this would not be the case. She continued to tell Emma she understood why Vern did not feel braces were a priority. She let Emma know that she was not upset with him because she understood his feelings, and she hoped Emma would do the same. Nancy emphasized that Vern was not necessarily wrong and that his decision was no reflection of his love for Emma. It was a simple disagreement that Nancy could not give in to.

Their two arcs separated. Nancy set aside part of her money each week and paid for Emma's braces. Vern did not like this at all; it took him several months to work through his resentment. But Nancy went about her life with the healthy realization that he had to be responsible for his own emotions. Although he never fully agreed with the course of action, Vern eventually came to accept it. Their arcs came back together and joined again into a power circle. An important lesson for Emma was that her parents did not allow the situation to become a triangle. They kept her in an insulated circle by letting her know their disagreement had nothing to do with her personally.

By confiding in Emma and explaining the situation to her, her parents have better prepared her to deal with conflict and disapproval. They have shown her logical and peaceful ways to solve disagreements. Emma has also learned not to take sides; triangles do not benefit anyone. They pull kids between parents and parents between each other. Nowhere is this more evident than in some divorces. And nowhere is it more important to be firm and responsible with discipline and united fronts than in blended families—ex-partners included! Most of us know many stories about ex-husbands and ex-wives using their kids against each other—unfortunately, this is often fertile ground for the triangle.

Viv and Walter divorced when their daughter, Jessie, was eleven. Joint custody was granted after a long and bitter ordeal. Jessie was repeatedly put in positions where she had to choose one parent over the other. For example, at Christmas the parents made Jessie pick where she wanted to spend the holiday instead of leaving her out of it and deciding it themselves. They did the same thing with her birthday.

> Viv asked things like, "You love me more, don't you, Jessie?"

> Walter would prod with, "Jessie, you wouldn't leave me for your mother would you?"

This poor child was put in a triangle that has probably been devastating to her. This type of selfish behavior on her parents' part is inexcusable. Divorcing families should consider professional advice during their transition—unless the parents are aware of the upcoming challenges and have the ability to behave in the best interest of their children.

As adults, we must take responsibility to work through our problems ourselves, not through our children. The triangles created in their lives can have horrible effects on them and on their future relationships. On the other hand, children of divorce should not be allowed to use parents and stepparents against each other either.

If you can't put your personal animosities with your ex-partner aside, then you should communicate through an attorney or other mediator. Children need the security that only your leadership and maturity can give. If you let them have power over you or your ex-partner (or new partner), you do them a grave injustice. Please, seek professional help if this a problem for you.

In blended, nuclear, and nontraditional families, relationships with teenagers are especially vulnerable to triangles. During the teen years our kids go in and out of circle shape so often that we must keep them even more insulated than before. Otherwise, we will allow them to draw us into triangular relationships.

This does not mean, however, that we give control over to our teenagers. They still need to know we are in control of the family, we make the rules, we enforce them, we draw healthy boundaries, and we let them suffer the consequences of their behavior.

Teenagers can have uncanny ways of jostling for control and doing the very things we dread the most. They can be irritating, worrisome, and ornery to the point where they dictate the mood of the entire family. It is absolutely necessary for their well-being, as well as for the well-being of the rest of the family, for parents to remain in control.

Teen Tyranny

Even the best teenagers can experience the moodiness and traumas of raging hormones, social distractions, performance pressures, and relationship challenges. By the time a child reaches high school he or she is pressured to be up-to-date on everything: future plans, sexuality, societal problems, political programs, financial savvy, fashion trends, and relationship issues. No wonder many teens frequently swing between optimism and despair. Kids face dozens of problems every day at school, on athletic fields, and at social gatherings.

Parents need to know these two things:

1. Most teens are bothered, at least sometimes, with mood swings and erratic behaviors that are natural for this period of life. These feelings are then enhanced by the pressures of today's fast-paced, demanding society.

2. They must be aware, observant, conscientious, and firmly in charge of their households.

Janet and James thought that all was going fairly well on their home-front. Their seventeen-year-old son, Aaron, was in his junior year in high school with no remarkable problems. Their fifteen-year-old daughter, Tami, was a freshman at the same high school as Aaron. Tami was somewhat more temperamental than Aaron, but she had not been in any real trouble.

Janet and James believed the moods, demands, and behaviors their kids were experiencing were small compared to some of the things other parents were going through. They figured as long as there was no alcohol or other drugs, sexual indiscretions, or situations of violence, their children must be all right.

However, late one Saturday evening, as Janet and James prepared to turn in, the phone rang. It was a sheriff's deputy, who told them that Aaron and Tami were in custody—he had said something about a party being busted. The conversation did not register with Janet beyond the notification that her kids were in jail. Janet and James got dressed and drove in shocked silence to the police station. As soon as they opened the door, the noise of many raucous teens struck them. Some amount of relief washed over them—at least it wasn't just their kids.

One-by-one and two-by-two, parents began showing up. It came to light that these were only sixty of the estimated two hundred teens who were caught partying at a remote county park. The rest of the party-goers had scattered off into the night. The police said there was so much beer, pot, and paraphernalia there—along with minors who were wildly under the influence of alcohol and drugs—they were left no choice but to haul the large group in to the station and charge them accordingly.

It was a long night for Janet and James. And the next few days dragged by very slowly. As the shock of the situation wore off, anger began to set in. Feelings of betrayal and disappointment followed closely behind. Then blame and shame demanded attention. Janet and James did not understand what had happened. Aaron and Tami involved in such a mess? They would be put on probation. There would be certain legal ramifications.

To make matters worse, when the family sat down together to discuss the incident, both Aaron and Tami grew sullen and defensive. They insisted that all kids did this kind of thing every weekend and that it was no big deal. Janet and James were appalled. How could they have been so blind?

As the parents began to discuss the circumstances with one another, all kinds of issues came to light. Janet and James inadvertently discovered many things about their teenagers they would never have suspected. When confronted, Aaron and Tami defiantly admitted the truth of several past experiences they'd each had. Aaron had been sneaking off regularly to a nearby city where he went to underground parties—he had done this for two years without getting caught. When his parents thought he was at high school football games and dances, Aaron was actually driving drunk on the highway or attending illegal gatherings. Tami had been dating a nineteen-year-old for seven months. She seemed proud of the fact that they occasionally smoked marijuana together.

The hurt was deep. Janet searched the kids' rooms after they left for school the next morning. She found beer in one of Aaron's drawers and what looked to her like what one of the deputies had called a "bong" for smoking pot on Tami's closet shelf.

James began to withdraw. He was so disgusted by what he found out about his children that he could hardly stand to eat at the same table with them, much less openly communicate with them. It seemed that every time Janet tried to talk with the kids she either ended up crying or screaming. The kids decided that since they had been "discovered," they would begin to act openly and not hide anything from their parents. Aaron skipped school several days in a row—and he didn't even bother to call the school to say he was sick. Janet got a call at work one day from the attendance secretary who said she didn't know where Aaron had been the past few days. Tami's midterm grades were horrendous. Janet grounded her, only to have Tami laugh in her face, grab her purse, and saunter out the door.

Finally, Janet could take it no longer. She had talked to the principal. She had talked to their pastor. She had tried to get James to open up. She had tried until she was nearly crazed to get the kids to cooperate. And now she would take care of herself—she went to a therapist and poured out her heart. After only a few sessions, Janet could see where she had missed many of the trouble signs in the months—and even years—before the kids were taken to jail. She also saw how she and James had allowed the teens to take control of the household.

As soon as the kids had hit adolescence and became more difficult to get along with, Janet and James gave in to their desires for the sake of family peace. They gave in to little things at first, such as allowing them to go out on school nights or date kids the parents did not approve of. Then the issues got bigger; in order to avoid ugly confrontations, Janet and James were more and more lenient with the children—many times beyond their better judgment. But the kids seemed happy, and Janet and James ignored any suspicions, convincing themselves they were just being overly protective.

The kids' desires then grew into demands. After the night of the busted party, Janet became willing to do anything to preserve even a few fleeting moments of harmony and peace at home. She clung desperately to the hope that her family could somehow go back to the way they had been. What Janet learned, however, in her several months of counseling was that she really would not have wanted to go back. Obviously, things were not as bright and healthy as she had thought at the time; but denying the symptoms of existing problems had only worsened them.

Janet realized that the biggest contributions she and James had made to their children's problems were . . .

○ Not making or enforcing rules.
○ Allowing the kids too much power and freedom.
○ Trying to avoid conflict.
○ Ignoring signs of trouble.
○ Not allowing the kids to suffer their own consequences.
○ Attempting to avoid reality.

When a parent is not the head of a household, teens are able to tyrannize the entire family and themselves. Regardless of their defiance, tears, anger, or antagonism, they may unknowingly want us to be in control, and they need us not to give up on them.

Of course, things are not always pleasant, convenient, or easy. But there are a few alternatives. If we allow our kids to pay the consequences of their choices and behaviors, we eliminate much of our own discomfort; this discomfort naturally transfers to them—where it belongs. Given their own painful consequences, teenagers will often resolve to take better care of themselves. This may not be in our timetable or appear in ways we prefer, but it usually does happen.

I can't remember how many times I saw my dad shrug his shoulders and respond to us kids—in one scrape or another—"If you're gonna play, you gotta pay." Thinking back, it would have been much easier for him to rescue us than to let us pay the price. But he did the right thing. Today I have two invaluable lessons from my father's wisdom:

1. I take full responsibility for my actions.

2. I know I can resolve my own problems. (After all, if my dad thought I could, then I guess I must be able to!)

"If You're Gonna Play, You Gotta Pay"

This seems like a good motto for every man, woman, and child. It applies to everything from a hangover to the national debt. And it most certainly applies to teenagers.

Make a concerted effort with your significant other to discuss what the closest natural consequences are to any given behavior or choice your teen makes, including celebrations and rewards for the positive! In fact, negatives can often be turned into positives with careful monitoring of consequences.

For instance, one day in high school, Adam saw another boy treating his girlfriend abusively. Adam told the boy to knock it off. The boy then turned his rage to Adam. Adam was a big kid but not a fighter by nature. When the other kid threw a punch, Adam pushed him to the ground. He did this three times, saying he did not want to fight. The fourth time the boy came at him, Adam swung a fist and connected with the other boy's jaw. Adam broke a little finger.

When Adam explained what happened to his parents, they were skeptical. But several others backed up Adam's story and proclaimed him a hero for being so chivalrous. Adam's parents didn't know what to do. They didn't want to punish Adam for helping someone, but they did not want to encourage him to fight either.

Adam's mother took him to the doctor for x-rays and to an orthopedic specialist. Everywhere they went, Adam was teased and then praised for his gallantry. Adam's parents decided the natural consequences of fighting would be for Adam to pay his own medical bills. This was neither punishment nor reward—simply a consequence. This was a highly successful plan. Not once, in Adam's three remaining years of high school, did he ever swing a punch again. Yet, on numerous other occasions, Adam was singled out as a person who stood by friends in need.

You should have only a few basic rules, which you enforce diligently and consistently. Rules for teenagers should generally involve respect, safety, and common sense—not only for themselves, but also for others. Remember, by the time you have teenagers you have given nearly all you can to them. Now is not the time to start clamping down; it is the time to start letting go.

If your teenager refuses to obey the rules or becomes belligerent, then you may have to let him or her really go—out the door. Do not allow the teen to tyrannize the family. Get professional help. There are many wonderful resources that help teenagers and their families. It is senseless to isolate yourself in a miserable and frightening situation. To find the resources in your area call your child's school, your doctor, clergy, an attorney, or a therapist. You can also call your local social services office or a telephone hotline for assistance.

Watching from a Distance

If things at your house are heading in the right direction, it is time to step back and watch. My mother was exceptionally good at this. From the time we were little, she would show us how to do something and then step aside. Our results usually weren't perfect—often not even very good—but she praised the effort and its outcome. I remember my first attempts at cooking, sewing, swimming, driving, and managing money. They were sorry attempts, but Mom made me feel worthy of each one.

My confidence grew, and now I take on most new experiences with excited anticipation.

Had my mother insisted on interfering, forcing me to do things perfectly, or rescuing me every time I was stuck, I never would have learned how to take care of myself. It can be very difficult to stand back and watch a teen pay the consequences of his or her actions. Rescuing is one of the biggest temptations for any parent.

For example, Janet and James could have let their children spend the night in jail. That would have influenced the kids more than all of Janet's coaxing. And it may have allowed James to express his negative emotions. Instead, he felt helpless and withdrew from the family.

Of course, it is unpleasant to allow our children to go through experiences such as these. But as parents, we must remember that our job—from the moment of their birth on—is to let our children go! They are not possessions for us to keep. They are separate persons. And if they are going to be able to function successfully in the world, they need to have practice being adults while under our watchful eyes.

By the time our kids are teenagers, we must . . .

- Detach.
- Observe.
- Correct only when absolutely necessary.
- Refrain from rescuing them.

Watching from a distance can be very hard. You may want to take the following quiz to see if you are allowing your kids to grow up or if you are constantly rescuing them.

Quiz: Are You Letting Them Go?

Circle **True** or **False** for each of the following statements as they apply to you:

1. If my son fell and broke his arm, I would help him up.
   True   **False**

2. If my daughter received an unfair grade on her report card, I would discuss it with her teacher.
   True   **False**

3. If my teen got a speeding ticket, I would pay for an attorney to represent her.
   True   **False**

4. If my son couldn't afford insurance for his car, I would pay for it.
   True   **False**

5. If my daughter needed to bring cookies for a dance at school, I would bake them.
   True   **False**

6. If my child forgot to take his lunch to school, I would bring it to him.
   True   **False**

7. If my teen got home late and didn't complete her homework, I would write an excuse for her.
   True   **False**

8. If my teen forgot to go to a dentist appointment that I was later billed for, I would pay for it.
   True   **False**

9. If my child were treated badly by the police, I would look into the matter.
   True   **False**

10. If my child were arguing with his friends, I would step in and help him settle things.

$$\textbf{True} \qquad\qquad\qquad \textbf{False}$$

Assessment

If you answered True to numbers 3, 4, 5, 6, 7, 8, or 10, you are likely rescuing. If your teen is picked up for speeding, *she* should pay for her attorney, not *you*. By doing this, she will learn to take the consequences of illegal behavior.

If your son is old enough to operate his own car, then he needs to learn how much it costs. If a child is old enough to go to a school dance, then she is also old enough to bake cookies.

If your son goes without lunch one day, he'll likely remember to take it in the future. If your daughter gets a zero on her homework, she will be more likely to complete future assignments.

If your teen has to pay for a missed dental appointment, he will probably remember the next one. And if you are settling arguments for your youngsters now, how will they handle relationship differences as adults? Think through these areas. By helping your kids too much, you are actually hindering them. Let them grow up.

Chapter Nine
Circling Above the Crowd

Watching our children make their own mistakes and pay the consequences is very difficult. We hurt for them. We want to save them from the agonies of life. We know in our heads this is impossible, but our hearts often betray us. Most parents, at one time or another, wish they could trade places with their children and suffer for them.

It is in the best interest of the children (as well as the parents), however, to rise and "circle" above them. We need to watch over our growing children from a higher position so we can remind ourselves of the bigger picture of life—the one that shows how challenge and hurt often contribute to stamina, character, growth, and perseverance.

If we can think ahead to what we give our children by letting them go, we will be able to watch their attempts at growing up with more confidence, patience, wisdom, and understanding. We can appreciate their efforts to try their own wings and be assured that, with practice, they will grow stronger and be more able.

Wobbly Wings

Nobody becomes an expert at anything without practice. Growing up is no exception. We can "circle above the crowd" and allow our children to try their own wings while we remain ready to help them find ways that will allow them to strengthen themselves for solo flights.

This should start at a very young age, and we should help them less and less as they get older. We need to encourage our children to be *interdependent* *with* us, not dependent *on* us. Interdependent means that we each have our own circle shapes—we all circle together but are not linked or dependent on others for our happiness or well-being.

We can insulate our kids within the power circles of our partnerships—and encourage increasing interdependence as they move from childhood to adulthood—by remembering a few basic principles.

1. Pull Rank with Love—And Often!

You're the boss. You pay the bills and provide the food, shelter, clothing, and emotional well-being for your kids. You can be their friend, of course, but you're not *just* their buddy. You are their source of security, sensibility, and survival. Firm leadership doesn't mean abuse—it means drawing clear lines between who makes and enforces the rules and who follows them.

2. Live According to What You Preach!

Don't tell your kids it's wrong to lie, cheat, or steal and then do so yourself. Don't shout about alcohol and other drugs with a beer in your hand and a bag of pot on your nightstand. Don't tell your kids it's immoral to sleep around and expect them to respect you if you're spending nights with different partners. When you do set a bad example—and you will—point it out, be accountable for it, say you are sorry (if that's appropriate), and make a vow to keep trying to do better.

3. Stand Firm on the Ground of High Standards!

Of course, we are all human and must accept that we have weaknesses and faults. We will make mistakes and do things we wish we had not done. But we must think carefully about lowering our standards too often. If we treat our children with high regard and expect the best from them, they will deliver the best and have high regard for themselves.

4. Practice! Practice! Practice!

No child is perfect. Help your children practice what they need to improve. Younger children can practice what they would do if a stranger tried to coax them into a car. Preadolescents can practice various scenarios: peer pressure to drink, smoke, vandalize, steal, cheat on school papers, or wrongfully tease others. Pretend you are in these situations with your children and let them practice a variety of possible responses.

As the teen years progress, you can role-play different ways of handling relationship issues as well: sex, date rape, disagreements with peers, pressures to do *anything* against their will, abusive adults, or violence. You can help them establish guidelines for when and how to seek professional help and how to set future goals.

Approach teenagers with a "We want to watch you from a distance" attitude and invite teens to practice using these suggestions:

○ Give your thirteen-year-old a homemade report card for weekly chores. Give rewards for various grade levels (A=4.0, B=3.0, C=2.0). Be sure also to honor the average effort (C). After all, most of us fall somewhere around average in life.

○ Tell your fourteen-year-old that he or she can invite five friends (so there are three pairs) for a dinner party. Have your teen do the planning, shopping, meal preparation, serving, and cleanup. (You provide the money, advice, and transportation necessary.) Allow the kids their privacy and let your child practice being a host.

○ Let your sixteen-year-old do the family grocery shopping and run errands for you. Give your teen signed checks to buy what you need. You will be displaying parental trust and giving your child some responsibility. If he or she is not doing so already, have your teen begin to schedule his or her own dental, haircut, and medical appointments.

○ Ask your seventeen-year-old to sit down with you when you figure out bills. Let your teen see how much it costs to run a household such as yours. Have him or her write the checks, balance the checkbook, file the receipts, ask questions, and offer comments.

○ Think of other things that young adults need to know to be able to take care of themselves and let them practice those things as you watch from a distance. Their wings will be wobbly at times, and they may not do things as efficiently or correctly as you do. But give them their space and allow them the dignity of making their own mistakes—we all have the right to mess up. With practice and a little coaching from you, your teen will be headed for adulthood with a lot more preparation, experience, and confidence.

Nosedives

Can you just sit by and watch your children take nosedives? Isn't it better to swoop in and rescue them from pain when you can? No! There are exceptions to every rule, of course, but your children will never learn to be independent with you sheltering them. It is essential that you come to terms with this fact. This doesn't mean that it is better to reject a child in trouble. It means it is best to stand back, take stock, and logically respond to situations. Choose the best course of action under individual circumstances.

Irene and Mel learned this the hard way with their daughter, Kelly. They began rescuing Kelly from consequences when she was only a little girl. If there was a problem at school, or something Kelly disagreed with, Irene and Mel would rush to the teacher (or principal) to take care of things. They complained, manipulated, and made excuses for their daughter until the school personnel could hardly stand to see them.

Kelly learned very quickly that all she had to do was whine, and her parents would charge in to protect her. Little did they know, they were setting up a pattern that would keep Kelly in their "nest" long after she should have been gone.

By the time Kelly was in junior high school she was so spoiled the other girls her age avoided her. Even her teachers were distant, fearing that Irene and Mel would target them with their wrath. Kelly became more and more demanding, surly, and uncooperative. Although Irene and Mel inwardly cringed from their daughter's unpleasantness, they continued to save and indulge her.

When Kelly entered high school, Irene and Mel were exhausted from the patterns they had created. Of course, they were not conscious of their contributions to Kelly's personality and problems; they just thought they were unlucky for having such a selfish daughter. They resigned themselves to tolerating Kelly until she graduated—then she would be on her own and their lives would be more settled and happy.

Wrong. After Kelly graduated from high school she became even worse. She went to college only to call home daily with her complaints and problems. Unfortunately, Irene and Mel continued to save her. They allowed her free use of their telephone calling cards and personal charge accounts.

When Kelly was thrown in jail for being drunk and disorderly, Irene and Mel drove six hours in the middle of the night to bail her out. They hired an expensive attorney to represent her. They soothed her bruised ego by agreeing with her that she had been unjustly treated by the police. They also told her the attorney would probably get the judge to at least reduce the charges.

Kelly quit school and moved home to take a break from the rigors of college life. Irene and Mel spent the next year trying to convince Kelly to do anything that would help her move away from home. They had grown accustomed to their privacy and were very anxious to get her out on her own again.

Finally Kelly took an interest in interior design and was promptly packed off to the best school her parents could afford. Halfway through the program, Kelly quit.

She said the institute's instructors did not understand her, and she could learn more on her own—she didn't need their stupid certificate of completion to make it. She was so obnoxious about her skills and potential as an interior designer that Mel allowed her to bully him into cosigning a loan for her to open her own studio.

Irene and Mel crossed their fingers; this had to help Kelly grow up. Within several months, however, Kelly had alienated the few customers she'd had, and the phone stopped ringing. Kelly walked away from the business—and the loan—without even a wince.

Mel had made a half-dozen payments to the bank for Kelly when she insisted she'd met the man of her dreams and coerced her parents into a wedding production that cost a big chunk of their savings. Irene and Mel were happy to do this; they hoped they had finally handed Kelly over to someone else.

But Kelly's marriage lasted only a little longer than her college years, and she ended up back on Irene and Mel's doorstep—this time with a baby. They took her in and prayed zealously that she would grow up.

Kelly got a job as a cocktail waitress at night. She refused to leave her baby at a stranger's house and convinced Irene and Mel that, since they hardly went anywhere anyway, it wouldn't be too much trouble for them to babysit.

Kelly liked to socialize after work. Often she would drag through the door just as Irene was putting the baby in the high chair for breakfast. Kelly then went to sleep. It was usually late afternoon before she woke up. Then it was almost time for her to start getting ready to go back to work.

Eventually, Irene and Mel resigned themselves to having another child to raise. For years, Kelly flitted from job to job and relationship to relationship. The baby almost always stayed with Irene and Mel when Kelly decided to try a live-in arrangement with a man.

> Kelly assured them that, "No man will ever want to marry me and raise my child if he hasn't had me all to himself for a while first."

When Kelly's daughter entered junior high school, she was a whiny, awkward girl whom the other kids couldn't stand. The cycle seemed to be repeating.

Mel died the year before his granddaughter graduated from high school. Irene clung to Kelly and the teenager with the tenacity of grief. Kelly and her daughter manipulated and used Irene until all her money was gone. Then they went their own way and left Irene to live by herself. Irene died a few years later, alone and lonely, with nobody to help her.

Not every parent rescues to the extent this couple did. And not every child reacts to rescuing like Kelly and her daughter did. But it is wise to take an honest inventory of your habits when it comes to your kids and their problems. From the time your toddler angrily pulls a toy from another child's hand, you should be aware of the power you have to influence his future.

Do you interfere? Do you coax and cajole him into better behavior? Do you punish him sternly? Or do you leave him and his little friend to work it out as best as they can? Do you rush over to correct your young one when she is learning how to tie her shoes? Do you insist that she color inside the lines? Do you chastise others for "making" her cry?

Do you go to parent-teacher conferences in a defensive mode—ready to let the teacher have it as soon as any criticism of your child comes out? Do you give lavish birthday parties or over-donate to youth athletics so that your child always looks good? Do you do the better part of your child's homework to ensure a good grade or presentation? Do you let him stay home from school if he doesn't have an important project done in order to buy him extra time? Do you make up excuses for him when he misbehaves?

What about your teenager? Do you screen calls for her? Do you confront her coaches for coming down too hard on her? Do you write excuses when she wants to skip school because of a test she hasn't studied for? Rescuing your kids from the nosedives of life may be one of the most destructive things you can do. How can our children develop self-esteem if they are not allowed to try, fail, try again, and succeed?

One of the most difficult things Paula and Don did was to not rescue their son, Zach, on his first Christmas away from home. Zach had been on his own for only a few months and wasn't managing his money well. At Thanksgiving Paula and Don loaned him money to come home, socialize during the long weekend, and get back to his apartment. Zach left with assurances that he was going to get a job and pay his bills, so he could enjoy a leisurely Christmas at home with his parents.

But he did not get a job, and he continued to spend money unwisely. As Christmas approached, Paula and Don knew they could not rescue Zach again. They told him they would not lend him money as they had at Thanksgiving—which still gave him plenty of time to "save himself."

But there was no change. By the time Christmas arrived, Paula thought her heart would break without Zach being home for the holiday. They got through it—not in the way they would have liked—but in a way where they could still enjoy their other children and each other. Zach did not like the situation any more than his parents did. He got a job right after his lonely Christmas and stuck with it. He started managing his money better almost immediately and began to make other decisions more maturely.

This made watching from a distance worthwhile. Paula and Don knew they had done the right thing by not intervening to loan Zach money. The same "don't rescue" policy goes for making payments, cleaning up overdrawn checking accounts, fixing troubled love relationships, ignoring bad grades, and for any other situation that you know is best handled by your child.

This is not to say that help, encouragement, support, and empathy are unnecessary; these are vital to the development of your offspring's confidence, self-esteem, and success. But rescuing teens, doing tasks for them, using power to influence the decisions of others in their favor, or punishing them into doing it your way will not help them mature into responsible adults.

A good barometer to gauge whether or not you are doing what's best for your child is your emotional level of involvement. Do *you* want her to make the cheerleading squad more than she wants it herself? Are you more infatuated with his girlfriend than he is? Do you pressure her to be homecoming queen or class president? Are you on committees or boards for the sole purpose of creating better positions for your children? Do you feel it's okay to try to buy off police, attorneys, judges, teachers, coaches, or friends by calling in favors with gifts or donations?

Listen closely to your emotions; often you will see the true motives behind your actions. For instance, *because* Paula wanted Zach home for the holidays so desperately, she knew something was out of balance. She knew her emotions were too involved in the situation to trust herself to make the healthiest decision for Zach. This is a common paradox of parenthood: what we want the most for our children may not be the best for them. We need to be scrupulously honest with ourselves in order to distinguish between helping and rescuing.

If it is difficult for you to accept the notion that what you have been doing for your children out of genuine love and concern isn't necessarily good for them, think ahead. Think of how much self-esteem and success you might be depriving them of by doing for them instead of letting them do for themselves.

Many of the most fulfilling things in life are the little victories we experience along our way. It seems that our rewards are much sweeter in circumstances where we feel we've paid our own dues. We circle more easily alongside our children and others when we feel as though we have earned our "places in the sun."

Aiming for the Sun

When our kids are out of circle shape, pulling on our individual circles, as well as the power circles of our partnerships, it can be very difficult to sort things out. It is particularly hard to get ourselves back on track in circular motion. One of the tricks I use to help me to do this is what I call "aiming for the sun."

When I find myself fretting and worrying over my kids, wanting to rescue them—when I know it is better to let them have their own consequences—I force myself to look beyond the present circumstances. I look at where they may be after they have made their choices, paid their dues, and succeeded in taking care of themselves. My "sunny" place is one where my own children are adults with happy lives of their own.

We all have warm and sunny spots in our daydreams—mental places where we and our loved ones are happy, well, and prosperous. Even if these places are only fantasies and never come true, they can still help us bear up in the midst of a crisis.

Jack is a good example of a person who aimed for the sun. Jack's ex-wife, Evelyn, spent many years using their two children, Maggie and Brent, to manipulate him. If he didn't do exactly what she wanted, she would tell the children hateful lies and exaggerations about him. He was torn between giving in to Evelyn's demands and fighting her for the sake of saving the children. It took a long time before he finally realized that for the children's sake he had no real choice but to do his best and aim for the sun.

He knew he couldn't rescue the kids from Evelyn's choices or behaviors. They would have to make up their own minds about their mother and about him when they were old enough to think through all the facts. Meanwhile he would make his own position clear and hope for the best.

When the children were ten and twelve years old, he spoke to them honestly, without badmouthing Evelyn.

> He said, "Listen, kids, I have been allowing your mother to tell me how to behave because I was afraid if I didn't, she would turn you against me, and I wouldn't see you anymore. I have to stop doing this. It isn't good for any of us. The truth is that I love you both very, very much. I would never do anything purposefully to hurt you. It is important that you ask me about anything that has to do with you kids and me—not anyone else—not your mom, your grandparents, or your friends.
>
> "If you think I'm mad at you or I've done something wrong, you must ask me about it. I will always tell you the truth. And I will never stop loving you for asking me about anything—no matter how touchy the subject is. For instance, I pay your mom money every month to help pay for your support. I do this because you are my children and I want to help take care of you. Sometimes your mom and I don't agree about how to spend that money, and we get angry at each other. But that has nothing to do with how much we love you two.
>
> "No matter what happens or how angry your mom and I get with each other, we will always love you. You two must remember this. And someday, when you are grown up, you will better understand the things that have happened."

When Jack felt as if he'd covered as much ground with Maggie and Brent as he could, he let go of the situation. He set firm boundaries with Evelyn and finally felt some peace of mind in his own life. He aimed for the sun by looking beyond the children's childhood to their adulthood. He imagined shared holidays where they would sit around the fireplace, laugh, and love one another. Jack made his mental images as detailed as he could and warmed himself with the knowledge that if he did what he knew was right, even if it was hard to do, the future would bear the fruit of his efforts. And his relationship with his children would flourish because of his perseverance.

Doing what we know in our heads is the best thing for our children and ourselves can be a great challenge when our hearts want us to do other things. It's much easier to give in to our children's desires than it is to stand our moral, ethical, or parental ground. But the fact is that we cannot always be the good guys. We must draw hard lines, take longer roads, and wait out situations many times throughout our parenting years. If we can think beyond the issue of the moment to our children's future, we will be able to share in the warmth of their "sun," also!

When we've done all we can for our children—when we've circled above the crowd; when we've allowed them to try their wings and practice solo flights; when we've let them take their own nosedives; and when we've looked beyond the moment and aimed for the sun; then we can concentrate on our own "nesting." We can live more happily and circle more comfortably in our own lives. We've given our children what they need to live full lives, and now they must make their own decisions about whether they will do so—and how.

Nesting in Confidence

Nesting in confidence does not necessarily mean that your kids are grown and gone. It means that you are trying to have the most love, joy and goodness that you possibly can within your family at the present moment.

The complications of trying to keep self, marriage, family, and relationships with others together are overwhelming at times. But living a healthy life means living while you're in the middle of it all. It means accepting yourself for who you are, faults and all. It means inner joy, despite the hardships and painful realities that are a natural part of living.

You can nest in confidence when you have . . .

O Provided the safest, most loving environment you can for your kids.

O Accepted the reality of the family formula multiple and the fact that you cannot escape the natural challenges that arise from multi-level relationships.

O Faced and eliminated the unwritten rules and unspoken vows you may have made with your children that are not necessarily healthy for them or for you.

O Made any changes in your dreamscapes that are necessary for you, your relationship, and your kids to stay in circle shape.

O Coped with the fact that you gave your children life, and now you must let them choose how to live.

O Taken responsibility for disciplining your children.

O Worked on any triangle relationships that are negatively influencing your family life.

O Taken back control when teens have threatened to tyrannize the household.

O Allowed your children to experience the reality of "If you're gonna play, you gotta pay."

O Practiced watching your children experience the consequences of their choices and behaviors from a distance.

O Let them try their own wobbly wings and practice skills for living.

○ Allowed them to take their own nosedives.

○ Helped yourself cope with crises by looking ahead and aiming for the sun.

Now you can accept that you've given everything you can to your kids. You have provided the power circle of your love so they can grow up as insulated circles. Regardless of mistakes you've made in the past, or those you may be making right now, you can start fresh. Everyone is human, and none of us has done a perfect job with our kids. But we have likely done the best we can.

You have earned the privilege to nest in the confidence that your children will enter adulthood fully equipped to take care of themselves. There will, no doubt, be times of trouble and pain, but all of you will be better able to cope with these times because of your efforts.

As we prepare to explore our relationships with extended families and others (the outer circles) it is important to remember that your inner circle (self); power circle (partnership); and insulated circles (kids); cannot live healthy lives if oval shapes of outer circles are pulling on you.

Before you go on to the final section of the book, you may enjoy the following suggestions for "feathering your nest."

Suggestions for "Feathering Your Nest"

Gather around a table and take turns answering the following questions. You may be surprised at the differences and similarities. You can see why family life does not always go smoothly; this is okay! Be sure that each member of the family is allowed to answer with his or her own feelings—NO judgment, correcting, or criticism! This exercise allows for a time of safe, open family communication that will help you get to know, understand, and appreciate one another:

1. How do you picture yourself in five years (school, lifestyle, friends, job, appearance)?

2. What is the one thing you like most about each member of the family?

3. Who is your hero or heroine?

4. What is your favorite time of the day? Why?

5. Why do you think there are so many social problems at this time in history (poverty, racial tensions, AIDS, problems in schools, violence, chemical dependencies)?

6. If you could live anywhere in the world for one year, where would you choose to go? Why?

7. What is the one thing you would most especially like to learn how to do but are too nervous or afraid to pursue?

8. What is your favorite animal? Why?

Part IV

Extended Families—The Outer Circles

This

Not this

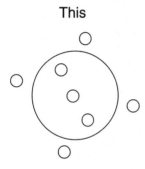

Chapter Ten
Planetary Alignment

Healthy living is often very challenging. It necessitates that we each diligently pursue our own circle shapes and healthy power circles in our relationships, as well as secure insulated circles for our kids. But it also means that we must pay attention to how we relate to those outside of our immediate families.

If we are pulled into oval eggs in our relationships with extended families, in-laws, friends, neighbors, or coworkers, we will likely suffer problems in other areas of our lives as well. It is important to look at how we are aligned with those outside our immediate family circles and assess whether these relationships are appropriate. When we know there are problems, we owe it to ourselves, our partners, our children, and others to form more healthy circles.

An adult's relationship to his or her family of origin can greatly affect the individual's life, relationships, and parenting. Every grown-up is somebody else's adult child. Therefore, everyone is somehow affected by the inevitable faults and failures that are unique to his or her particular family. This does not necessarily mean there are terrible problems in everyone's background. But there are nearly always negative issues and influences that are unavoidable and have passed from generation to generation. One family tree may be riddled with alcohol and other drug dependency. Another may be plagued by violent tempers or struggles with depression. Still others are burdened with an inability to express love, affection, or encouragement.

We must accept this fact: *no one is immune to problems*. Therefore, it is best for us each to take responsibility to look for those issues that are unique to our family. It takes a conscious effort to stop negative cycles and learn better ways to live.

Somebody's Adult Child

Genni is forty-four years old. She and Mac have been married for twenty-three years. They have three children: Lisa is twenty-one, Ian is eighteen, and Nick is sixteen. They have resided in the same medium-sized city on the East Coast ever since Lisa was born. Both extended families live within a six-hour drive and frequently interact with each other.

When Lisa began junior high school, Genni and Mac's marriage started to show signs of strain. Things got so bad between them that Genni felt the need to seek therapy to help herself work things through. Genni says:

> "When I first went to therapy, I thought the problems were somehow all my fault. Mac and I had been married fifteen years, and in many ways I felt as if we were strangers.
>
> "In therapy, I immediately began to have breakthroughs in regard to some of the roots of my problems. One of the first things that came up were my feelings toward Mac in regard to his relationship with his family. There was so much hurt and hostility stuffed inside me that it was just waiting to explode. I had been aware of resentments and irritations regarding Mac and his family, but I didn't realize how deep the problems went.
>
> "For example, when the kids were little, I wanted to spend holidays at home. Instead, Mac always insisted we pack up the troops and go visit his relatives. I don't know how many years I dragged diaper bags, playpens, high chairs, and babies from his parents' to his aunt's and to his grandma's house—both sides of the family. By the time the holidays were over, I was so exhausted and grouchy that I could

hardly stand myself, Mac, or the kids. Looking back, I don't know why I ever went along with this. I guess I was just young and insecure.

"The holiday scenario wasn't the only thing, though. It seemed like every time something came up that had to do with Mac's family, he put the kids and me on the back burner. We had to meet their expectations—no matter what our needs were. I used to think I was just a jealous, possessive wife. But when Lisa became a teenager and grew more active with her social life (which included boys) and school activities, I could see that Mac wasn't going to change. It appeared that he was more concerned with his relatives than with his own teenage daughter. I started to fight him.

"And that was the beginning of a long period of battles and heartache. Inside I really hoped that if Mac were pressed, he would do what I thought was right for the kids and me. But this didn't happen. I remember one time when Lisa was to be honored at a basketball team banquet. Mac and I were to sit at the head table with her. This was a very important occasion for Lisa. But Mac chose to go to his aunt's eightieth birthday instead. That was the last straw. The day after the banquet all I could see in my mind was the hurt in Lisa's eyes from the evening before. That's when I called the therapist and made an appointment.

"In therapy, I realized that my hurt and anger were understandable, considering the circumstances. I confronted Mac with it. He acted as though I were crazy. I backed down at first. But as the therapy progressed, I could see that in healthy marriages the husband and wife put their relationship first, above either extended family.

"I know now that the first fifteen years of our lives were colored by Mac's relationship with his parents. He passed up opportunities for promotions because they meant transfers—he didn't want to live far away from his family. We sacrificed private family vacations because we always spent our time off down South with Mac's family. I can remember being hurt many times when Mac considered his family of origin before me and his own children.

"When I first confronted Mac with my feelings about the situation, he didn't see anything unusual at all about his relationships with his family members. In fact, he said I was odd for not putting my extended family in a more prominent place in my life. The longer I was in therapy, the more I saw that Mac and I were polarized on our views of adult-child responsibilities and relationships with extended families. I loved my parents, siblings, and other relatives. But my husband and children came first. If I was to be there for my own household, then I couldn't be driving six hours back and forth between our parents' homes for every family get-together and mini-crisis.

"When my father had open-heart surgery, I was at the hospital and stayed with him and Mom for a week after he came home. I stayed with my sister for several days after her husband was killed in an auto accident. I go to important events, such as graduations and weddings for my nieces and nephews, when they don't conflict with things that are important for me, Mac, or our kids. I think my priorities are balanced and that Mac just carried things too far.

"I wish I would've been more confident in the beginning. Maybe things wouldn't have gotten so far out of hand. As it is, it took until Lisa graduated from high school for us to find a common ground with our extended families. I have had to make some compromises, too. There were things that bothered Mac that he'd never told me because he felt foolish and guilty. For instance, my family is not very affectionate. Mac comes from a family where they hug and express their love verbally. Mine didn't. Mac felt slighted by my uneasiness with open affection and love. I always thought people just knew that you loved them. I didn't think I had to say it or show it.

"As I made more effort to say and show my love to Mac and the kids, there was great improvement in the overall feeling in our home. We became more relaxed and upbeat. I have learned a lot about inner fears and hurts that I had left over from being raised in a family deprived of unconditional love and acceptance. It was as if we were to know by osmosis that our parents loved and approved of us. I guess I grew up accepting this as a fact, but it never quite felt right in my heart.

"Mac helped me see how wonderful it is to express love and affection freely. In return, I helped him see how vital it is for partners to put each other and their children first. Now we have mutual understandings, goals, and a family style all our own—a combination of the way his family and my family did things. We have taken the good from both our backgrounds, eliminated as many unhealthy things as we can, and taken on new ways of relating as we've learned them.

"I hope that as our children become involved in serious relationships, they will do the same. I only hope that Mac and I can give them a head start on their adult-child issues by letting them know what we've been through. We want to save them from some of the pain caused by our lack of knowledge and wisdom.

"In fact, we are very careful to tell Lisa, Ian, and Nick that we don't know everything and that we keep learning things all the time. I don't want them to feel the burden of having parents who are afraid to be less than perfect. I think if Mac and I had been consciously aware that neither of our families had all the answers, we would have been more likely to seek our own way as a couple."

Genni and Mac are very fortunate. Many couples go their entire lives without digging any deeper than the surface for the effects of their relationships with extended families. You do not have to be the victim of physical, sexual, or mental abuse to have conflict about issues that stem from your childhood.

It only makes sense that combining two different backgrounds will create friction. It is necessary to work through problems in order to compromise or create new ways of doing things if both partners are to feel loved, respected, and cared for. In turn, the power circle of the couple will be better equipped to insulate the children in a family circle of strength and harmony.

If children feel that they take second place to their grandparents, aunts, uncles, or cousins, they will likely develop a driving inner need to prove themselves worthy of your love and acceptance. If you do not express love and acceptance, your children are likely to act out in whatever way possible to get your attention.

If these ways are negative, of course your attention will be negative through discipline and disapproval. Then your children will feel even more unworthy of your love and acceptance. The cycle viciously continues until somebody, somehow, digs in, looks honestly at the situation, takes steps to stop the cycle, and creates a new way for the children to feel loved and accepted.

So even if your adult child issues seem to be slight compared to the blatant problems you hear on talk shows and read in books, you and your children can benefit greatly from your own "self" work related to your family of origin. Healthy boundaries are often difficult to establish when it comes to extended families. We have all heard horror stories about those whose relationships with their parents are so far from ideal that the problems are almost cliché:

○ Grandparents are notorious for spoiling their grandchildren.

○ Mothers are infamous for butting in where they don't belong.

○ Fathers are known for overprotecting their daughters or placing too high expectations on their sons.

If we are to live as healthy, loving, and fulfilled round circles with our extended families, then we must each take responsibility and initiative for resolving our individual problems. Dysfunction is not always a clearly defined problem. What is extremely painful for you to cope with may be a breeze for someone else and vice versa. But we can all benefit from probing into our own hearts and from the personal growth that comes from looking at our unique issues.

Problems for individuals and family groups may also arise from friendships outside the family circle. One partner may be unable to be assertive with a friend. The other spends too much time away from home with friends. The children may have friends that one or both parents do not approve of. Regardless of the specific situation, friends outside the family can have a great impact on the emotional climate of the home. Often we must find creative ways to confront unpleasant circumstances and let others know the rules of our household.

Somebody's Friend

Marilyn and Steve had been struggling with the next-door neighbors for years. For the sake of good will, Marilyn and Steve had made the Andersons feel too welcome at their home when they first moved in. The families got together frequently at Marilyn and Steve's for pool parties, backyard barbeques, and holidays.

The Andersons, delighted to have neighbors who were also good friends, told all sorts of stories about past neighbors who had been snobbish, reclusive, or cold. If Marilyn and Steve had listened more closely, they would have heard a common denominator in all of the relationship problems: the Andersons. But wanting to settle in on a positive note and being lonely in a new town made Marilyn and Steve ignore the warning signs. They rushed headlong into personal friendships with their new neighbors.

Several months later, problems began to crop up. At first they were little things: the Andersons made comments here and there about overhearing an argument between Marilyn and Steve; about seeing Marilyn and Steve's kids swimming with friends other than the Andersons' kids; about noticing when Marilyn and Steve had another couple over to visit; and about wondering why Marilyn and Steve hadn't answered their phone when both cars were in the driveway.

Marilyn and Steve tried to ignore the possessiveness they sensed and write off any irritation they felt in the name of getting along. But soon, the Andersons were getting on their nerves so much that they began to dread any contact with them. Rather than confront the situation, they withdrew more and more from the friendship with lame excuses as to why they couldn't get together.

Marilyn and Steve knew they'd made a big mistake. But they weren't sure how to correct it, short of selling their home and moving. They decided that Steve would try to talk to Bill Anderson. He would say that they needed to spend more time alone as a family as well as widen their circle of friends in the new community.

> After Steve approached Bill one Saturday, he stormed into the house angrily, "That S.O.B.! He is the most pompous ass I've ever seen!"

> Marilyn was shocked. "What?! What did he say?"

> Steve mocked, "Oh, just that if we don't appreciate all they've done for us, and if *we* choose to be so ungracious of their hospitality, then *they* certainly do not want us for friends!"

Marilyn couldn't believe her ears. A friendship that had started out with such good intentions and enjoyable times couldn't end on such a sour note. She went to talk with Norma Anderson to explain that she and Steve simply needed more space. She told her nicely that little things—like knocking on the door before walking in, asking beforehand to use the pool or to borrow the lawn mower—would go a long way toward easing the tensions they felt.

Marilyn was back home in less than fifteen minutes. She was so angry her face was red and her hands trembled as she told Steve what happened.

> "She had the *nerve* to tell me I was no longer welcome on her property and that I should please make sure the children know the same goes for them! Those people are lunatics!"

> Steve shook his head, "I guess it doesn't pay to get too close to people."

In some ways Steve was right. It is not wise to get close to others that negatively influence your entire household. It is not healthy to allow others to impose on your family's time, energy, or possessions. It is better to set clear boundaries at the beginning of friendships than to risk unspoken boundaries being crossed. This is not to say that you shouldn't have close, loving friendships. But these friendships simply should not usurp your family's relationships.

Fran and Lori's friendship got out of hand also and caused serious damage to Fran's marriage. Fran told Lori *everything* about her personal life and her relationship with her husband, Paul, and her two teenage children. She shared private things about her sex life, secrets from the past, and betrayed confidences Paul and the kids had entrusted to her.

Paul began to resent Fran's friendship with Lori. He complained that Fran put Lori before him and the kids. He told Fran several things about Lori that he didn't like, and Fran, in turn, repeated what he had said to Lori. Lori was hurt and became very upset. Without Fran's knowledge, she sent a vengeful letter to Paul. In it she used examples of very personal and private things to prove to Paul that she would use her powerful relationship with Fran to turn Fran against him if he wasn't careful.

Paul could not believe the letter's contents. He had no idea that his wife shared such intimate details of their personal lives with Lori. He felt betrayed, used, and unimportant. Fran, on the other hand, had thought that *all* women shared such private things. During her childhood, she'd overheard her mother and other women talking about their husbands and children in great detail. Fran had no clue that what she was doing was harmful. And she was certainly disappointed in Lori. Everyone in this situation learned some tough lessons about trust, priorities, and loose tongues.

There is a great difference between sharing confidences with friends and betraying family secrets. For example, you might share with a close friend that you and your spouse are having sexual problems and ask his or her advice. This does not mean that you should ever ridicule your partner's sexual performance.

You may lean on a close friend for help when one or another of your children is in trouble. That doesn't make it okay to criticize your child in front of the friend! It is very important to respect the feelings and confidentiality of others. We are all human and most of us find it hard not to discuss others occasionally, but that is entirely different from betraying the personal confidences of family members or friends.

You may find it helpful to develop some ground rules your family can use to evaluate whether extended family or friends are receiving too high a priority. Living in a healthy family is easier when you periodically monitor what's going on in your life, your relationship with your partner, your parenting, and your friendship with others.

Running Your Own Lives

Olivia and Norm base their decision for keeping immediate family relationships in healthy perspectives with others on the following guidelines:

○ Our public and private faces should be as closely integrated as possible. If we find that we are much nicer to, or more accepting of, those outside our family, we will make a conscious effort to balance ourselves.

○ We will remind ourselves that we are the number-one priority with one another by having a special family dinner once a month.

○ We will cast secret ballots and vote on whether to attend extended family get-togethers and other social gatherings. If there is a tie, or if it is an event that the parents feel is very important, then there will be further family discussion and a chance for everyone to voice an opinion.

○ If the parents disagree on the importance of attending an event, they will either go alone, go with the kids, flip a coin, or take turns doing what the other wants.

○ We will do all we can to be sure that the majority of us feel good about family decisions. But it is clearly understood that parents lead the family; their word must be final when there are impasses.

○ We will practice dealing with relationship challenges outside our family circle by role-playing. For example, the kids can practice what they will say to a playground bully, a steady they want to break up with, or a friend who has hurt them. The parents can try ways to turn down unwanted invitations, ask for raises, or express anger with those who have tried to take advantage of them.

○ We agree that we are each responsible for ourselves, our choices, and our behaviors. We are also responsible for our relationships with others. If someone outside the family is causing trouble within the family, then we agree that we must work together as a unit to solve the problem.

○ We understand that as parents and children we will always be connected, and therefore, we will try to love, understand, nurture, and accept one another. This extends to any future additions to this family through marriage, birth, or adoption. However, it is also understood that when the children in this family are adults, their first priority will be to their own future families. This will be respected, honored, and encouraged.

○ We believe that each of us has the power and ability to cope with life in positive and successful ways. We will take responsibility to meet our own needs and will not expect others to meet them for us. We will work hard to provide a healthy family environment that enables each of us to be fulfilled.

○ Although we are a single family circle, we will also be concerned about—and reach out to—others outside our home. We recognize the importance of being connected to others.

Olivia and Norm found that living within these beliefs eliminated many of the disagreements and problems they remembered from their own childhoods. They felt that giving their children a strong family circle and insulating them within it provided the security for each child to grow into the person she or he was born to be.

Of course, there are no guarantees that any of our kids will grow up to be happy, healthy, and successful adults. After all, they will make choices—some good and some bad—for themselves that are beyond our control. But as parents, we can provide as much insulation as possible between our families and unhealthy influences outside the family.

No matter how civilized we are or how desperately we want to draw boundaries without conflict or confrontation, others will sometimes refuse to respect our wishes—they will refuse to mind their own business. When this happens, we can best resolve situations as quickly as possible by being well prepared.

Making Others Mind Their Own Business!

Annie's boss is a good example of someone outside the immediate family circle who insists on butting in where she doesn't belong. Annie has worked for the same company for twelve years. Martha has been her boss for five. Martha is the kind of woman who has a definite opinion about everything. She tells Annie constantly that Annie allows her husband, Evan, too much control over her life and that Annie is too soft with her kids.

Annie, however, is just fine with the status quo and resents Martha's presumptuous advice. In addition to verbal input, Martha has taken liberties to manipulate Evan and the children. On one occasion, Annie's daughter chose a dramatic piece to recite for a speech contest. Martha did not think the piece merited a grand performance, and she bullied Annie's daughter to change her piece. Annie told Martha that she thought this was wholly inappropriate and asked the woman not to interfere with her children again. Martha acted hurt and barely spoke to Annie for days. In fact, she made it very hard on Annie at work. Annie had nowhere to turn.

In another instance, Evan came early to pick up Annie from work and surprise her with a romantic dinner for two. He had gone to great effort to leave work early and arrange time to spend with his wife. When he walked in the office, Annie was down the hall in the copy room. Evan told Martha what he was up to, fully expecting her to be supportive. But

Martha snorted and told him men just didn't understand that women didn't like having plans made for them. She also told him that Annie would be needed at the office until late that evening.

Completely taken by surprise and dejected, Evan left the office immediately and went home without questioning Martha. But when Annie arrived home at the usual time, he knew he'd made a big mistake. As he shared with Annie what had happened, she burst into tears.

"That's it! The old bag! I'm handing in my resignation tomorrow! She can't do this to me anymore!"

Evan was half supportive and half terrified. Annie made very good money, and they depended on her income to pay the mortgage. What would they do if she couldn't find another job? They couldn't live on one income without suffering financially.

Annie stomped around the house and fumed all evening. She thought about the other disadvantages of leaving her job. Besides making excellent money and having good benefits, Annie valued the relationships she had with her coworkers and liked her job.

As Annie calmed down, she thought about her options. She could try to look for another job on her own time. She could try to speak with Martha. But that had never worked in the past. Why should it be different now? Different, Annie thought. What could *she* do differently to make Martha mind her own business? Annie sensed this was the key—*she* had to handle things differently, not Martha.

Annie hardly slept that night as her mind buzzed with details of a plan that would make Martha mind her own business. She could hardly wait to carry it out! In the morning, she shared the plan with Evan. He thought it sounded like the best shot she had at solving the problems with Martha.

When Annie got to work, she asked Martha to go to lunch with her. Martha, who rarely got asked to do anything, was delighted—although she looked a bit skeptical. Annie then made a phone call and anxiously watched the clock the rest of the morning.

When noon rolled around, they went to an upscale restaurant where Annie was a regular. The waiter approached their table. He asked if they had made their selections. Annie nodded.

As soon as Annie and Martha had ordered, the waiter rolled his eyes and said, "Really? I don't think those are very good choices."

Annie looked at Martha. Martha's eyes were wide with surprise.

She blurted, "Why not?!"

The waiter looked back calmly and said, "I just don't think so. That's my opinion."

Martha sputtered, "But we don't care about *your* opinion! We want you to take our orders!"

The man shrugged, filled the order ticket, grabbed the menus out of the ladies' hands, and walked away without another word.

Immediately Martha said, "Can you believe he did that? My word! We must report him to his boss!"

Annie raised her eyebrows, "Really? For having his own opinion? I thought you were a champion of everyone having a right to express their opinions."

"Well, yes, but not to run right over people with them!" Martha stuffed her napkin onto her lap with a self-righteous, "Hmpf!"

Annie didn't say a thing. She watched as a young man approached their table with two pitchers in his hand.

He turned first to Annie and then to Martha. "Would you ladies care for plain ice water or lemon?"

Annie and Martha both requested lemon.

The young man grimaced slightly and said, "Hmmm. I would've guessed you two for plain. Are you sure you wouldn't rather have plain?"

Martha looked up at him with a jerk of her head, "Yes, we're sure! And I'll thank you to keep your opinions to yourself!"

The young man peered down at Martha, "Well, excuse me, but I think I have a right to my own opinion!"

Martha glared at him and then turned to Annie, "Have you ever seen such a thing?!"

Annie nodded to the young man who poured water in the glasses and left. Annie waited quietly until he had gone.

"Actually, Martha, I have. And that's one of the reasons I asked you to have lunch with me. I wanted to discuss this with you privately."

Martha looked wary. "What are you talking about?"

"Well, I think any of us get irritated when others try to tell us what to do. I certainly get upset when you tell me how I should behave with my husband and children. It's not for you to say, Martha, any more than it is for the waiter to tell us what to eat or the busboy to tell us which water to drink."

Martha began to blush. At first she looked embarrassed and then angry.

"You set me up! You tricked me and humiliated me in front of those people!"

Annie was quick to respond, "No! I only told those two that I was playing a joke on a friend. They know nothing else about us! And, Martha, I would like it if we could be friends."

Martha was not to be placated immediately, "Well, I think this is a dirty rotten trick!"

Annie said, "I think it was pretty rotten to tell Evan that I wouldn't like his surprise and that I had to work late yesterday when you knew that wasn't true."

Martha stammered, "Well, I, uh, I suppose I, uh . . ."

"You had no right?!" Annie offered.

Martha hung her head, "Yes, I suppose that's correct. I shouldn't have interfered. But you shouldn't have brought me to lunch under false pretenses!"

"Martha, I agree that I manipulated you. And that's part of what I wanted to demonstrate—it doesn't feel very good to be pushed around by someone else. But I really did want to discuss it in private, outside the office."

Just then the waiter came and graciously served their lunch without a hint of provocation. Martha visibly relaxed. She smiled at Annie.

"You know, I am very impressed! You may have tricked me, but it certainly was effective. I guess I haven't taken a look at myself in a long time."

For the rest of the lunch, the two women ironed out their differences. Annie had prepared a list of boundaries that she intended to set with Martha and expressed them calmly. She had a tactful signal she would give Martha when there was interference going on.

Martha agreed to try to respect Annie and her family. She apologized for the pain she had caused them. Annie accepted the apology and stressed that the details of their luncheon and arrangement would remain confidential.

It took several months of renewed efforts, but eventually Martha did mind her own business and respect Annie's boundaries. Others may have handled this situation differently. They may or may not have been as receptive to such a scheme as Martha. Annie took a great risk, but traditional avenues had not been successful with Martha. Considering the stakes, Annie decided it was worth the try. Fortunately, it worked.

You may not need to go to such extremes to make your point with those who don't respect your beliefs, needs, or desires. However, it is imperative that you work through situations where others are pulling on your personal, relational, or parental circle shapes. You must learn how to handle others who continually butt into your business.

The same rules apply to everyone:

○ Accept
○ Respect
○ Circle

Accept others for who they are, respect their privacy and their boundaries, and circle *with* them. Don't try to link together in suffocating imposition! We all need room to work, rest, and play!

Freedom to Work, Rest, and Play

Once you've dealt with your own family of origin issues, put your relationships into healthy perspectives, are satisfied that you are running your own life, and have coped with interfering people, you can relax and enjoy life! Live moment by moment. Each new day brings different opportunities, challenges, and experiences. We are free to choose whether we will fight, ignore, tolerate, accept, or change each negative experience we encounter. We are also free to choose how we feel about these experiences. Are we afraid? Angry? Resentful? Resigned? Helpless? Hopeful?

Nobody escapes pain, but we can all choose how to deal with it. Being emotionally healthy means making a conscious decision to relax and enjoy life as much as possible and to gracefully accept bad circumstances we cannot change.

In the next chapter we will look at how to cope with really tough situations and explore ways to survive them while retaining our circle shapes. But before you go on, you may want to try the following exercise to spot areas in your life where you are linked to others who are pulling on your circle and forcing you to become an oval egg.

Exercise: Balancing All the Plates

Using the following scale, rate your relationship with each of the people listed below.

1 ——————2 ——————3 ——————4 ——————5

Least Pleasant   **Most Pleasant**

Mother   Partner's uncles
Father   Partner's cousins
Sister(s)   Neighbor(s)
Brother(s)   Boss(es)
Mother-in-law   Coworkers
Father-in-law   Friends
Sister(s)-in-law   Partner's friends
Brother(s)-in-law   The public
Stepparent(s)   Children's teachers
Other Steprelative(s)   Doctors
Grandparent(s)   Attorneys
Aunts   Clergy
Uncles   Fellow committee members
Cousins   Others
Partner's aunts

Evaluation

Were most of your numbers on one side of the scale or the other? Look for patterns. Are there certain groups of people with whom you do not have pleasurable relationships? Your partner's family? Your own? Are you middle-of-the-road all the way? Why do you think this is? Are you unwilling to commit to meaningful relationships?

Answer these questions and think through how you balance relationships with those outside your immediate family. If you listed mostly 4s and 5s with a sprinkling of 1s, 2s and 3s, then your relationships seem to be fairly well balanced. If there are specific people with whom you have trouble, you may want to work things out for your own peace of mind.

Chapter Eleven
When Life Slaps You—Punch It Back!

To live happy, fulfilled lives we need to accept the fact that we will experience pain and suffering. We must also face our heartbreaks, cope with them as best we can, and move on! We must choose to probe our lives for past injustices, present burdens, abusive behaviors, unnecessary rage, unwarranted fears, obsolete defensiveness, and any other negative aspects of our lives that are preventing us from getting the most out of life.

This means living with the **FACT**s:

> 1. Facing
> 2. Accepting
> 3. Coping
> 4. Time healing

You may have been abused as a child, but in order to leave dysfunction behind, you must face, accept, cope with, and allow yourself time to heal from this personal reality. Is it truly possible to recover from life's hardest knocks? Is it feasible to bounce back after we've gone bankrupt, had a son killed in an accident, been divorced four times, or acquired a disabling disease? How can we expect to relax and enjoy life if our teenager is addicted to alcohol, if we have just lost our job, if our relative is in jail, if our child has run away, or our parent is dying of cancer?

Obviously, no one enjoys such things. However, there can still be joyful moments amid tragic times. The number of joyful moments depends largely on our attitudes. So prepare yourself to get an attitude. And when life slaps you—punch it back!

The Hard Knocks

Celeste and Val were devastated when they found out their twelve-year-old daughter, Tricia, had a terminal illness. She was expected to live only to age sixteen.

> Celeste says, "The first few days we were numb with shock and disbelief. Naturally, we did not want to accept that Tricia would die. She was hospitalized when the doctors told us about her disease; it wasn't until we brought her home a week later that we began to feel the reality of the situation."

> Val adds, "For months, I tried to deny that Tricia would actually die. I kept thinking there was some awful mistake and that at any time the doctor would call to tell us Tricia's test results were wrong. But when her hair started falling out from chemo treatments, I couldn't pretend any longer.

> "I will never forget the day the full magnitude of the situation broke through to my conscious mind. I was reading the morning paper, and as I turned the page I saw a little girl's picture in the obituary column. She was about the same age as Tricia. She had died in a boating accident. As I read the details, tears started streaming down my face and soaking the paper. Celeste came into the room a few minutes later, and we sobbed in each other's arms for an hour."

Tricia died the week before she was to start the eighth grade. There was a tremendous amount of love and support from her family, her friends, and the community. Celeste and Val were overwhelmed by the thoughtfulness of so many people. Though it helped ease their pain, Celeste and Val discovered that the lives of others outside their immediate family soon began to return to normal while their own lives were forever scarred.

The days passed by slowly in the first months following Tricia's death. Celeste often thought she would lose her mind. Val sank into the sorrow of searing grief. Nobody else could take away their despair. They couldn't even do this for each other.

Tricia has been gone for five years now. Celeste and Val still miss her acutely, but they have faced her death, accepted it, coped with it, and allowed time to heal many of their wounds. They have gone on to create new lives for themselves.

Celeste explains, "The second year after Tricia died I felt I had no right to be happy or live a full life. I guess I thought somehow I owed it to Tricia to be sad and to continue grieving. It's as if I believed that I would be less of a mother if I kept living without her."

Val adds, "Yes, and I thought that any parent should mourn a child's death forever."

Celeste says, "And then one day I sensed a miniscule change in my attitude. It was the moment I began to become a whole person again. I was standing on the patio with a broom in my hand when two hummingbirds came to the feeder. I stood still and watched them—I noticed the blur of their tiny wings beating rapidly and their beautifully decorated green feathers enhanced by ruby-red throats. There was such wonder in those few seconds. It was a reminder to me that even the smallest thing can bring pleasure and awe, but only if we open our minds.

"From then on I deliberately looked for little things to be joyful about or thankful for. I began to put myself back together one moment at a time—like grains of sand filling up a jar. The fuller I got, the more I realized I had feared that being happy would somehow diminish my love and memory of Tricia. But it has been just the opposite. The more love and goodness I extract from life and the more I let others outside the family in, the more I feel at peace."

Val had a harder time rejoining the mainstream of life, and he withdrew emotionally after Tricia's death. For more than three years, his life consisted of getting up, going to work, coming home, eating, watching television, and going to bed—all in a robotic, somber fashion.

Val says, "I think I forced myself to keep going in a tightly structured way—I was afraid to let myself feel again. I thought I would fall apart and never recover. But a little over a year ago I had an experience that sort of restarted my life.

"I was at the grocery store and the checker was a girl that Tricia had gone to school with. Before I had seen her former classmate, I hadn't realized that Tricia would've been seventeen. Seventeen. When I left the store I couldn't get my mind to stop racing. I kept thinking of all the things Tricia had missed—all the silly, wonderful, and painful things of adolescence.

"And for some reason it really bothered me that she never got to go to a prom. Without even realizing what I was doing, I drove to a florist's shop, got a long-stemmed red rose, and drove to the cemetery to lay the rose on Tricia's grave.

"That was the day I finally let myself feel the full impact of her death. I babbled on for hours to her grave and said all the things I had left unsaid during her illness and after her death. I never told Celeste or anyone what was really going on inside me. That day, I finally accepted her death and my feelings of inadequacy. My helplessness in the face of Tricia's death and the fear of not being able to control the situation had crippled me. It left me paralyzed.

"But after that day at the cemetery, I began to let myself be human again. Little by little I opened up to Celeste. I allowed myself to reconnect with some friends and coworkers. I made myself take on new challenges that forced me to make new acquaintances and to renew my life. I learned to play tennis and took night courses at the community college. The past year has been much better."

Tricia's older brother, Brian, reacted differently. He began drinking heavily after Tricia was diagnosed with her illness and hasn't quit since. His life has progressively grown more out of control, and the family has had to face this additional tragedy.

> Celeste remarks, "We each have our choices to make. Brian chose to escape reality. But he just postponed it. The alcohol may take some of the hurt away for a few hours, but eventually sobriety comes and the pain returns. But the pain is so much worse than it was before he started drinking, he can't get enough liquor down him to numb his pain.

> "Brian has been in and out of jail twice, in a car accident, lost three jobs, and God knows how many friends because of his addiction. He's in debt up to his eyebrows, won't have a driver's license until he's twenty-five, can't get health insurance, and has all but cut himself off from anyone who even comes close to loving him. How much more painful can reality be than that?"

Celeste and her family have certainly had their share of pain, but they learned how to work through it, and so can you. One of the best ways to deal with the hard knocks of life is to let reality work for you, rather than trying to run from it or fight it.

Reality Works!

Many of us never have to face the horror of losing a child. But life throws many other obstacles in our way that we must get around. Problems with finances, relationships, parenting, health, extended family members, careers, and other issues pull us out of circle shape from time to time. We never have to look very far to find someone who is dealing with greater challenges or problems than we are at any given time. But the reality is that this does not make our personal crises much easier to deal with or any less relevant to us. The truth is, we can sympathize with others who have heavier burdens, but our pains do not disappear simultaneously—and rightfully so.

Without challenging realities, we lose the uniqueness, depth, and character that we gained from growth by trial. Here is where we need an attitude. We can remind ourselves that each crisis we survive makes us stronger, more mature, and more able to cope with future hardships.

Celeste and Val feel that Brian's alcoholism has been more difficult to deal with in some ways than Tricia's death.

> Celeste says, "When Tricia died, I knew I couldn't do anything to change it. Regardless of the devastation, I knew I didn't have a choice in the matter. But with Brian's problems I wanted so badly to do something—anything—to help him get better that I became an emotional wreck."

> Val nods sadly, "We sat up through so many nights and put our heads together trying to think of a way to help Brian. It wasn't until this year when we started going to Al-Anon meetings that we discovered the best way to deal with life's hardships: face reality and deal with it head-on."

> Celeste concurs, "Our reality is that Brian is the only one who can take responsibility for himself. If he chooses to drink himself to death then that's the way it will have to be. We can't do anything to control that. What we can do is take care of ourselves.

> "There are no guarantees for any of us. It doesn't matter who we are, where we come from, how much money we make, or what race we are—we will all encounter hardship and loss along the way."

> Val says, "Our faith in God and the love of others are the things that have helped us to cope with our own harsh realities. Our new friends at Al-Anon have been such a blessing. I don't understand how anyone can make it without leaning on others to love us back to wholeness when we've fallen apart."

> Celeste has tears in her eyes as she says, "In many ways the reality that we've had to accept is that we can't bring Brian

back to his healthy self any more than we could bring Tricia back to life. It's a tough thing to deal with, but we are making it—not without scars—but we are."

None of us escapes some wounding and scarring from reality, but we can use our hurts to our advantage. Reality works! If we will allow our personal tragedies to lead us, it is possible to discover richer, fuller lives. We will meet new people, connect with others in more meaningful ways, learn to fine-tune our priorities, develop greater appreciation for the wonders of life, have more empathy, and be more passionate about living to our maximum potential.

Accepting reality gives us resilience. Resilience offers better opportunities for positive living. When you have been hurt by reality, it is perfectly normal and even beneficial to burrow into your own sorrow for a while. But then it is time to take action.

Dusting Off

After a period of suffering, it is important to use the FACTs. Make a commitment to face, accept, cope with, and let time pass in order to heal. There comes a time when you must pick yourself up, dust yourself off, and move away from the danger of being swallowed up by self-pity.

Joyce and Ray experienced extreme difficulty using the FACTs to help them face their harsh reality. After twenty-three years of service with an aerospace company, Ray was laid off. Since he had not yet reached retirement age, he sacrificed many of the benefits he and Joyce had planned on receiving and got very little severance pay.

Although the layoff was a stressful shock to them, Ray and Joyce were convinced that things would be okay. They'd tighten their belts and wait out the few weeks they thought it would take for Ray to find a job. But the few weeks passed. The aerospace industry was crippled badly by a lagging economy, and there was a surplus of engineers with Ray's qualifications. A few months passed with no job prospects. Ray and Joyce began dipping into their savings. A few more months slipped by and they began to feel anxious.

Ray and Joyce had ridden the wave of the prosperous eighties to the crest. They had bought their house at a good price early in the decade. They got an equity loan in 1986 and used the money for several personal luxuries. They added a master suite to the house, refurnished the children's bedrooms, put in a swimming pool, went to Europe for a family vacation, and put money down on an expensive car. The future looked very bright.

When the youngest of their three children entered high school in 1987, Joyce went back to work as a nurse practitioner. She also made good money, which allowed them to pay college tuition for their two older children. After a year of Ray being jobless, they could barely keep their heads above water. They were two and three months behind on their bills, and their savings was almost gone. They did not even have enough money to pay for the kids' upcoming tuitions or to think about putting their youngest child through college next fall. Full-fledged panic overtook them.

With Joyce's wage, they were barely making the mortgage payments and feeding the family. They couldn't refinance at lower interest rates or get another equity loan because their house now was appraised for less than they owed on it. Things looked very grim.

> Joyce relates, "Right after Ray was laid off, I convinced myself that it was nothing for me to be upset about. I denied the seriousness of the situation and acted as if it would just be a matter of days before things got back to normal. As the weeks and months passed, I tried to make myself keep believing everything was all right, but reality started creeping in. The bills were past due and collectors started calling. My paycheck looked very small.
>
> "After a while I was nervous whenever the phone rang. I refused to answer the doorbell for fear it was someone serving a collection notice. I was also afraid to go out in public—I was afraid I would see someone we owed money to and be embarrassed.
>
> "The only relief were my rides home from work. I would turn up the radio and fantasize each day that this would be the day

I'd walk through the door and Ray would say, 'Honey, I got the most fabulous job! It's just a matter of catching up, and we'll be right back on our feet!'

"Of course, that day didn't come. Things just kept getting tighter and more strained. Ray got depressed. He was so discouraged at one point he considered committing suicide."

Joyce's eyes still reflect the despair she felt then. She goes on to say their car was repossessed and their credit cards cancelled. They lost their home and finally filed for bankruptcy.

"Everything just snowballed. Looking back, I see there were things we could have done to save the house and relieve some of our pressures. But at the time, we were in such denial that we just wanted to hold on to the slim possibility that things would return to the way they were. The day we finally accepted the reality of our situation was the day we got on our feet, dusted ourselves off, and really began to cope with our situation."

Joyce and Ray coped by starting over completely. They stayed in the same town so that their youngest child could graduate from high school. They sold their house and managed an apartment complex in return for free rent. Ray did the managing, and Joyce's salary paid the rest of their scaled-down living expenses. After their youngest graduated, they loaded what possessions they had left and moved to a little town in the Northwest where Joyce had some relatives.

Her relatives gave Ray good references at an electronics firm and he finally landed a job. His salary was less than half of what he previously made, but he was working. Slowly, one day at a time, his depression started to lift. He opened up to some of his coworkers and found them to be very supportive and understanding. Through their care and friendship, Ray began to regain his self-esteem.

Joyce and Ray have been in their new town for only several months. But they are starting to feel hope for a good future. Their two oldest children got federal grants and low-interest loans to help them finish school. The youngest is going to a community college in their new town and lives at home. Joyce works as a nurse at the local hospital and thoroughly enjoys her new circle of friends.

> She says, "We could've given up. There were days when I thought our marriage was over, and I had nothing left to live for. As long as I tried to deny and fight reality, it got the best of me. Only when I faced, accepted, and chose to cope with reality did I begin to feel hopeful again.
>
> "I learned that hope is only good, however, if you are willing to combine it with action. We were passively hopeful for too long—it cost us our home, our car, and our credit. But as soon as we picked ourselves up and took action, we began to see results. Now that some time has passed, I'm able to take what is good in our lives and leave the past behind. It's gone now, and I'm just thankful I don't have to live with it anymore."

Joyce brings up an excellent point. Hope *must* be combined with action to get results! Life can deliver some awful blows. We can choose to sit and wait for things to change, or we can get up and do something for ourselves! We can't solve our hardest problems overnight; that's why we must be willing to let time pass. While time passes, we can be helping ourselves heal a little bit at a time. We realize the best progress and most fulfillment when we learn to take each day as it comes and live it as joyfully as we can.

Living in the Moment

Living fully requires that we live in the present moment. This doesn't mean we cannot learn from our past mistakes or plan for the future. It means getting the most out of each day. If the day offers only pain and despair, then we can get something from it—we can let it happen and tuck the pain away to help us become stronger. Or we can use it as a catalyst to look for things to be thankful for. Or we can choose this time to allow others to love us and help take care of us. The point is this: don't waste your life sitting around waiting for it to happen!

We know that good and bad exist side by side; we also know that we will not go through life without experiencing some of both. We waste our lives when we allow ourselves to be devoured by fear and worry. Can you think of a time when your fear or worry prevented something bad from happening or forced a good thing to come about? Did worry over a lump in your breast ever make it go away? Have you ever worried so much over a sick child that the fever broke? Has a child's fear of the dark ever stopped the day from ending or speeded up the passing of night?

Living in the moment means using the FACTs of reality to your advantage. All we have is the present moment—no one knows how much time he or she has left on this planet. We should be concerned about living positively (in circle shape) with our partners, children, extended families, and others.

Of course, we all want to be happy. We want to experience inner peace and joy all the time. We know that this is impossible in a fallible world. We also know that without the contrast of painful experiences, we wouldn't recognize joy. The one thing we all seek, and the underlying motivation that drives us, is *love*. We all want it. In fact, the need for love is so great, many people will try anything to get it—even use destructive, bizarre tactics. Like a plant that twists and turns every which way to grow toward the sun, people creep, crawl, climb, bend, shoot up, and intertwine to find love.

Life can slap us, but we can punch it back. We can face reality, accept the hard knocks, cope with ensuing problems, and allow time to heal our wounds. We can also enjoin hope with action and dust ourselves off and live joyfully in the moment. But without love in our lives, we lose our resilience. We will wither and falter and lose our motivation. It is of ultimate value for us to find our circle shapes and circle lovingly with others so we can lead healthy lives.

In the last chapter we will explore the facets of real love, what happens when our lives spin out of control, how others can help us while we maintain our separate circles, and how we can empower ourselves to enjoy the kaleidoscope of life's adventures.

Before you go on, please take a few minutes to take the following quiz. It will help you determine whether you've allowed the problems in your life to submerge you in self-pity. Self-pity is a poison that needs your immediate attention. It can rob you of much joy and peace if you do not take action against it.

Quiz: Are You Submerged in Self-pity?

Circle **True** or **False** after each statement below as it applies to you.

1. My life is wonderful!
   > **True**   **False**

2. My life has its ups and downs.
   > **True**   **False**

3. My partner is an anchor around my neck.
   > **True**   **False**

4. I'm so unlucky I would lose a winning lottery ticket.
   > **True**   **False**

5. Someday my ship will come in!
   > **True**   **False**

6. My relationships have good days and bad days.
   > **True**   **False**

7. If I could just get one or two problems off my back I'd be fine.
   > **True**   **False**

8. I've tried to be happy.
   > **True**   **False**

9. When I'm in trouble, I need time to myself to think things through.
   > **True**   **False**

10. Others have more love in their lives than I have.
    > **True**   **False**

11. My family of origin did not have any problems.
    > **True**   **False**

12. Sometimes I worry about what I may be doing wrong as a parent.
    > **True**   **False**

Assessment

If you answered True to numbers 1, 5, 7, and 11, look very closely at your attitude toward hardship. You may be living in denial and trying to find the magic key to a fantasy kingdom of happiness that does not exist.

If you answered True to numbers 2, 6, 9, and 12, you seem to be balanced in your life. You know there are ups and downs, yet you still find pleasure and hope. Keeping your balance will help you live more positively. Keep it up!

If you answered True to numbers 3, 4, 8, and 10, stop and look around you! Notice the beautiful sunsets. Feel the silk of spring air on your face. Watch changing cloud shapes in a summer sky and work on not feeling sorry for yourself. You may want to seek professional help. Get a positive attitude, and slap life back!

Chapter Twelve
Circles in Motion

As we've seen throughout this book, moving on to a healthier life is largely dependent on the following:

○ Assessing our needs and situations honestly.
○ Deciding to change or eliminate our negative feelings and attitudes.
○ Devising practical plans to help ourselves.
○ Taking the actions necessary to fulfill our plans.
○ Letting time pass to allow ourselves to heal.

As you know, life is constantly changing, and the process is not always pleasant. But we can be extremely adaptable if we give ourselves a chance. In fact, if we look back at the tremendous amount of ground we've covered together in this book, we will see that we've circled together.

1. We must each be responsible for ourselves.

2. We must all face our emotional insecurities accounts.

3. We must create healthy boundaries.

4. We must come together as separable arcs in committed relationships.

5. We must not handcuff ourselves to our partners.

6. We must be willing to renegotiate our partnerships.

7. We must spin cocoons of love around our children.

8. We must discipline our children and be strong leaders in our families.

9. We must allow our children to take the consequences for their choices and behaviors.

10. We must align and monitor relationships carefully with those outside our families.

11. We must be prepared to punch life back when it slaps us.

12. We must be accountable for loving ourselves and others.

Life is always in motion, and we must not wait for love to come to us or for others to make us happy. We must reach out for our own love and happiness.

Love Is Always in Motion

Real love is not sedentary or stagnant. It is continually evolving and moving. It offers us the most rewarding and challenging moments of our lives. We can be full to the brim with warm feelings of love between us and our loved ones. We can be pushed to the wall with the demands of a troubled teen or partner, but at all times, love is in motion.

Kathy and Reece had been married for fourteen years when they decided they wanted to call it quits. They thought they just didn't love each other anymore. They tried to be philosophical about the situation as they worked with their attorneys to agree on property, child support, and custody issues.

As the months went by, they realized they were communicating more effectively now than they had in the last few years of their marriage. Kathy found herself looking for reasons to invite Reece over to discuss matters that could have been left to the attorneys or worked out over the phone. Reece was more than happy to rearrange his schedule to see Kathy.

One evening Reece came over for dinner. As they sipped their coffee, Kathy said she felt more benevolent toward Reece now than she had when they were married. Reece admitted that he, too, felt more cooperative than before.

They speculated on these unusual feelings for over an hour. It finally dawned on Kathy that because they separated and were pursuing a divorce, they were actually *doing* something about their relationship.

Reece agreed, "I think over the years we got too passive about our love. And by not working to keep it alive, we allowed it to go dormant."

Kathy said, "Yes, and without the pressure of daily irritations to compound our problems, it's easier to see why we loved each other in the first place."

Kathy and Reece ended up reuniting. They renegotiated their marriage and will soon celebrate their twentieth anniversary. They are happier now than when they first met.

Understanding that real love is always in motion—doing for your self, your partner, your children, and others—is the key to resolving many relational problems. You may be lying beside your partner looking at the moonlight, and it may appear that love is still, but it is merely quiet. The *doing* is in your companionship, your resting, and your unspoken emotions.

Sitting by the side of a sick child, stroking her forehead is loving her comfortingly. Patting the hand of an aged grandfather is loving him gently. Baking brownies for a school function is loving your kids. Taking time to attend a community play your mother is in is showing her your love and support. Forgiving yourself is loving yourself.

The circling of love does not have to be loud and overt. It can be soft and subtle in hundreds of little ways. But it is always on the move. Many of us mistake "lip service" for the real thing. We say, "I love you," flippantly to others, and we sign our names, "With Love." But what are we *doing* to demonstrate our love? And what *is* love anyway?

Love is the foundation of all that is good in our lives. We must pay our respects for this wonderful, life-giving force by doing for its sake—love will grow by leaps and bounds when we are willing to do our parts.

What good does it do to say we love and then act selfishly and rudely? Is it possible to say we love our children, yet not protect them? Is it right to say we love our partners and then treat them unkindly? Is it desirable to say we love a friend and avoid that person when he or she is in trouble?

Oftentimes we face challenges that only love can help us through. We may be in debt, sick, confused, or abandoned. We may not be able to make the money we need, to get healthy, to think clearly, or to bring a loved one back. Sometimes when our lives are out of control, the only thing that will help us survive is love.

Spinning out of Control

Sometimes bad things happen that we cannot prevent or predict. Our lives spin out of control for one reason or another. We may be fully accountable for ourselves, have healthy partnerships, well-adjusted kids, and sound relationships, but then life pounds us with problems that seem insurmountable. When we are in undesirable situations, we must face, accept, cope, and let time pass to heal ourselves. We aren't being singled out, punished, or abused by life when we find ourselves knocked down; bad things happen to perfectly fine people.

Tara's doctor found a lump in one of her breasts when she was thirty-eight. She then had a mammogram and a biopsy that confirmed it to be malignant. Immediately she had a radical mastectomy. Tara was devastated. She was engaged to be married. Her fiancé, Tim, added to the trauma with his inability to cope. Tara's life was a mess. After several weeks of chemotherapy, Tara got tough. She fought the physical side effects of the treatment, as well as the fear, depression, mental fatigue, and severe strain on her relationship with Tim.

Just when Tara was feeling stronger and her hair was starting to grow back, Tim left her. She found a note on the table when she got home from a doctor's appointment that said he just couldn't handle it. He said he wasn't proud of himself, but he knew couldn't make it through the months of her healing, reconstructive surgery, and recovery.

She was completely desolate. Besides all the other things she had to deal with, she was now thrown into a precarious financial situation as well. Although her job was waiting for her, her paid sick leave had run out, and she wasn't ready to return to the office. Tim's salary had been supporting them. She had no idea how she was going to manage.

At first, Tara allowed hopelessness to swallow her up. She stayed in bed for three days—although she hardly slept at all. She didn't answer the phone or go to the door. She got up only to go to the bathroom. She ate very little and did not bathe.

On the morning of the fourth day, Tara noticed Hattie, an older neighbor who lived next door, walking outside her window. Their eyes met briefly, and Hattie signaled Tara to open the window. Tara didn't feel as if she had much choice. When only the screen was between them, Hattie begged Tara to please open the front door and let her in. Tara grudgingly obliged.

Letting Others Help

Hattie didn't say a word. She leaned forward, took Tara in her arms, and hugged her. Tara was taken off guard. Her pent-up emotions finally built up and spilled out in sobs of panic and despair. Hattie held her for several minutes before she gently pushed Tara away and led her into the living room. Hattie sat down beside Tara on the sofa.

> She said, "I saw Tim loading his things in the car the other day. Then I noticed he hasn't been back, and I haven't seen you out since. Tara, I got worried about you. I don't want to pry, but I do want to help you."

Tara nodded her head weakly and said, "Yes, Hattie, I need help desperately. I don't know what to do. I feel so lost and alone."

Tara's tears started afresh. Hattie stroked her hair and crooned to her.

"There, there. You aren't alone. I'm here now, and I know lots of other people who care about you and who will help you through this."

As Tara's tears slowed and her sobs turned into hiccups, Hattie went to make a pot of coffee. In just the few minutes it took to get it started, Tara fell asleep on the sofa. Hattie tucked an afghan around her carefully and then took a look around. The house was a mess, and the curtains were closed. It was a gloomy sight. While Tara slept, Hattie worked. She changed the bed linens, picked up, washed the dishes in the sink, cleaned the bathrooms, and baked banana bread.

When Tara awoke, Hattie opened the drapes and some windows. The place looked bright and cheery. The two shared some banana bread, and for the first time since Tim left, Tara felt a small ounce of hope. Hattie coaxed Tara into sharing her feelings. Tara told her story while Hattie listened silently, with abundant compassion. Tara felt so safe and cared for—she hadn't felt this way in months.

She had lived right next door to this grandmotherly woman for nearly a year and probably hadn't spoken more than two dozen words to her. Now Hattie was here to help her. It felt good to be connected to someone who she sensed genuinely cared.

Although Hattie did one of the most helpful things any person can do for another—LISTEN—she also set love in motion by doing several other things for Tara over the following weeks.

O Hattie and Tara talked about Tara's financial situation. Tara decided to rent out one of the three bedrooms in the house to a college student to help pay the bills. The other room she rented to a woman in return for the woman's keeping house, cooking, and running errands for Tara. Hattie then helped Tara comb through the house and gather things for a garage sale. This netted almost three hundred dollars.

O Hattie prompted Tara to approach her boss and explain her situation. Although she still wasn't strong enough to work five days a week, she could go in for a few hours each day and take some projects home.

O Hattie told Tara she would be happy to keep up the yard and flowers until Tara was able. She also offered to help Tara wade through the mountain of paperwork that had accumulated from medical bills and insurance forms. This was a huge relief to Tara.

O Hattie took Tara to the hospital when it was time for reconstructive surgery. She visited her daily and brought her home when she was released. During the several days following, Hattie organized a brigade of people from Tara's office and the neighborhood to visit, bring food, and do errands for Tara.

O One of Tara's coworkers felt that although Tara was healing physically, emotionally she was still reeling from the aftermath of the mastectomy and Tim's desertion. The coworker asked Tara if it would be all right if her pastor dropped by to visit Tara. Tara did not object. She knew she needed help to stabilize her emotions, but she didn't think she could afford therapy, so the pastor's visit was highly welcomed.

O The pastor agreed to visit Tara for one hour once a week. Tara objected to taking so much of his time gratis. At first he insisted it was perfectly fine for him to counsel her without compensation. But when he could see that Tara needed to feel as though she were pulling her own weight, he struck a deal with her—he would counsel her now, and when she was fully recuperated, she would donate an equal number of hours to help at his church. Tara brightened considerably and gladly accepted.

O One of Hattie's friends who had a mastectomy years before came to visit Tara. The woman was kind and empathetic. She addressed many of Tara's fears and concerns; she knew what Tara was going through and was a great comfort to her.

O Tara's boss organized a "come and go" coffee one Saturday. Friends and coworkers stopped by to enjoy refreshments and visit Tara. This way she didn't get too worn out, and her spirits were lifted by the company.

Fueled by all the love and support she received, Tara began restoring her circle shape. Within three months after her reconstructive surgery, Tara was back at work full time. She then resumed her social life. She realized she had been so dependent on Tim that she had completely shut other people out of her life. Now she knew that a healthy relationship involved interdependence with others as well. She was circling in motion and felt good about herself for the first time in nearly two years.

Maintaining Dignity and Integrity

Tara had extensive help from neighbors, friends, and coworkers to help her regain control of her life. Many things less dramatic than cancer or the desertion of a loved one can cause life to spin out of control temporarily. You may be a new mother who needs a break or a grown child whose parent recently moved into a nursing home. You may be a new retiree who feels displaced and fearful of the future. You may be pushed out of your circle shape by a crisis with a child, problems at work, declining health, problems with a loved one, finances, or any other life challenges.

Allow yourself to receive help when you need it. None of us can get through life alone. We need others so we can enjoy life. But accepting help doesn't mean giving ourselves up to others. Our goal is to recover our own circle shapes. Maintaining dignity and integrity is vital to wellbeing. This necessitates doing for yourself what you can and allowing yourself to accept help when you need it.

Accepting help does not have to mean enmeshment with others or giving up healthy boundaries. In fact, it is in everyone's best interest to keep *some* distance. When people start feeling used, too obligated, suffocated, or overburdened, resentment and anger begin to surface.

Notice how Hattie helped Tara, but she also included others so there was a network of aid—no one person was expected to carry the full load. Tara also helped by trying to solve some problems on her own: renting her rooms, working at home, and trading counseling for volunteer work at a local church. These activities enabled Tara to keep her dignity and integrity while still getting the help she needed.

At the same time, none of the caregivers linked destructively with Tara or told her what to do. Each person's actions were aimed at expediting Tara's return to health and independence. These were circles in motion of real love—doing for a peer, while at the same time respecting her separateness.

The great healing adventure of finding a healthy lifestyle is one of excitement, joy, tremendous effort, fear, frustration, success, failure, courage, weakness, and strength. There are rarely two days alike. Life is not static; it will continue to spin whether we're in circle shape or not. The quality of our lives depends solely on how we handle being fully accountable for loving ourselves and others.

Each of us must determine whether we will get the most out of our lives and our relationships. We can stand in one place and let life spin around us, or we can put ourselves in motion and contribute to the brilliance, depth, and positive energy of our world.

Enjoying the Kaleidoscope of Life

There are several things that people who love and live life to the fullest have in common. Some of these are listed below to help you to get the most from the kaleidoscope of your journey to a positive, healthy life.

○ They are passionate about many things but rarely fanatical about anything.

○ They share themselves genuinely—strengths, weaknesses, and faults.

○ They value themselves and others highly.

○ They allow themselves and others plenty of space to grow, change, and love.

○ They appreciate nature and the environment.

○ They accept the fact that everyone makes mistakes, fails, and has troubles.

○ They take action to help themselves and others through difficult times in life.

○ They expect the best from others—and often get it.

○ They avidly seek knowledge, wisdom, and understanding.

○ They see aging as a normal process and not an enemy to be battled.

○ They know their children must be allowed to grow up and become their own best selves.

○ They do not harbor prejudices or make harsh judgments.

○ They have great compassion for others.

○ They believe in love and go to great lengths to preserve it—without sacrificing their integrity.

○ They believe in God or a higher power and live by their faith.

○ They remain optimistic—despite the hard knocks and ironies of life.

○ They set healthy boundaries for themselves and respect the boundaries of others.

○ They accept their share of trials and tribulations.

○ They are "students of excellence" and strive to better themselves and their relationships.

○ They offer their hearts in love, trust, joy, and eager anticipation.

The kaleidoscope of life demands that you take charge by continuously turning it in order to see all the intricate colors. You can be the kind of person you want to be. You can fulfill your own dreams and create the kind of life you want. But you must be prepared to experience pain along with joy. Life offers no promises or guarantees. Take a careful look at the following suggestions for loving others.

Suggestions for Loving Others

Bearing in mind that love is always in motion, do one or all of the following for extended family, friends, neighbors, or coworkers, as appropriate:

1. Buy postcards. Address them to people you care about. In the space for messages, simply write, "I love you," and sign your name. Then be sure to mail them.

2. Send a letter every day for a week to a loved one or someone you know who is ill, going through a divorce, grieving a loss, or facing a hardship. A greeting from you may just be the lifeline he or she needs at this very challenging time.

3. Make a list of people you have been meaning to contact. Call one person on the list each week (perhaps each month if there are several long-distance phone calls to make) and check off the names as you go.

4. Buy a little gift for someone you care about and spontaneously share it with him or her. It may be as simple as buying your high school buddy a certain brand of gum you used to chew together, or bringing a friend a flower that is reminiscent of a special event you shared.

5. Plan to bring a friend, neighbor, or relative a dessert, or even an entire meal, just for the sake of letting him or her know you care.

As a final exercise, you can use the forms that follow to create your own "master plan" for life, including one-, five-, and ten-year goals to help keep you on the right track. This is the most important exercise, so make sure you take the time necessary to complete it fully.

Final Exercise—Making a Master Plan

Fill in the following blanks by listing your strengths, weaknesses, needs, and goals. Be as concise and honest as you can. It is important that you examine these with a thoughtful eye. For example, if one of your weaknesses is math, then you will need to consider whether becoming an accountant is really a good goal for you. On the other hand, if one of your strengths is getting along well with people, you may want to consider choosing a career in public relations or human resources.

If you are a reclusive person but work in a busy doctor's office, you may want to consider starting a transcribing service for physicians from your home. This way you can maximize your strengths (business knowledge, experience, and contacts), minimize your potential weaknesses by fulfilling your need for a more private, quiet environment, and meet your goal to continue earning money doing something you're adept at.

Strengths

1._____

2._____

3._____

4._____

5._____

6._____

Weaknesses

1. _____

2. _____

3. _____

4. _____

5. _____

6. _____

Needs/Goals

1. _____

2. _____

3. _____

4. _____

5. _____

6. _____

When you are ready, fill in the one-, five-, and ten-year plans with things you can do to maximize your strengths, minimize your weaknesses, meet your needs, and achieve your goals. Write everything—nothing is too far-fetched. What do you hope to be doing in one year? Where do you see yourself in five years? How do you think your needs will be different in ten years? Exercise your imagination and dream your power!

One-year Plan

Ways to:

Maximize Strengths	Minimize Weaknesses	Meet Needs/Goals

Five-year Plan

Ways to:

Maximize Strengths	Minimize Weaknesses	Meet Needs/Goals

Ten-year Plan

Ways to:

Maximize Strengths	Minimize Weaknesses	Meet Needs/Goals

After you have filled in your charts, go back to the one-year plan and begin to identify ways you could start doing some of the things listed. See what happens in the first few weeks. Are you doing more things that appeal to you? Are you feeling better about yourself and more hopeful about the future? Are other possibilities coming to mind? If so, you're headed in the right direction.

As you exercise personal choices and desires, you may notice you have a more optimistic and energized attitude. Keep your plans in a drawer, file, frame, or folder and follow through with them. As you meet your needs and achieve your goals, you will be surprised to see how many of your plans actually do come together.

Now that you have learned how to move on to more positive, healthy relationships, it's time to take action. Get out and start enjoying life. I wish you well in your endeavors and hope you find the peace, love, and happiness you deserve.

BIBLIOGRAPHY

SELF—THE INNER CIRCLE

Bepko, Claudia, and Jo-Ann Krestan. *Too Good for Her Own Good*. New York: Harper & Row, 1990.

Bradshaw, John. *Healing the Shame that Binds You*. Deerfield Beach, Fla.: Health Communications, 1988.

Cloud, Henry. *Changes That Heal*. Grand Rapids, Mich.: Zondervan, 1992.

Friedman, Sonya, with Guy Kettelhack. *On a Clear Day You Can See Yourself*. Boston: Little, Brown & Company, 1991.

McWilliams, John-Roger and Peter. *You Can't Afford the Luxury of a Negative Thought*. Los Angeles: Prelude Press, 1991.

Mellody, Pia, Andrea Wells-Miller, and J. Keith Miller. *Facing Codependence*. New York: HarperCollins, 1989.

Minar, Barbra. *Unrealistic Expectations: Capturing the Thief of a Woman's Joy*. Wheaton, Ill.: Victor Books, 1990.

Peck, M. Scott, M.D. *The Road Less Traveled*. New York: Touchstone, 1978.

COUPLES—THE POWER CIRCLES

Augsburger, David. *Sustaining Love: Healing & Growth in the Passages of Marriage*. Ventura, Calif.: Regal Books, 1988.

Chapman, Steve and Annie, with Maureen Rank. *Married Lovers/ Married Friends*. Minneapolis: Bethany House Publishers, 1989.

DeAngelis, Barbara. *Are You the One for Me?* New York: Delacorte Press, 1992.

Hendrix, Harville. *Getting the Love You Want*. New York: HarperPerennial, 1988.

Paul, Jordan and Margaret. *Do I Have to Give Up Me to Be Loved by You?* Minneapolis: CompCare Publishers, 1983.

Smalley, Gary, and John Trent. *The Language of Love*. Dallas: Word, 1988.

Tannen, Deborah. *You Just Don't Understand Me: Women and Men in Conversation*. New York: Ballantine Books, 1990.

Wiener-Davis, Michelle. *Divorce Busting*. New York: Summit Books, 1992.

KIDS—THE INSULATED CIRCLES

Anonymous. *The New Dare to Discipline*. rev. ed. Wheaton, Ill.: Tyndale House, 1992.

Dobson, James. *Parenting Isn't for Cowards*. Dallas: Word, 1987.

Johnson, Carolyn. *How to Blend a Family*. Grand Rapids, Mich.: Zondervan Publishing House, 1989.

—————. *Forever a Parent*. Grand Rapids, Mich.: Zondervan, 1992.

McDill, S. R., Jr., and Ronald D. Stephens. *Raising Safety-Smart Kids*. Nashville: Thomas Nelson, 1993.

Paul, Jordan and Margaret. *Do I Have to Give Up Me to Be Loved by My Kids?* Minneapolis: CompCare Publishers, 1993.

White, John. *Parents in Pain*. Madison, Wis.: InterVarsity Press, 1979.

Wright, H. Norman. *The Power of a Parent's Words*. Ventura, Calif.: Regal Books, 1991.

EXTENDED FAMILY—THE OUTER CIRCLES

Cloud, Henry, and John Townsend. *Boundaries*. Grand Rapids, Mich.: Zondervan Publishing House, 1992.

Cramer, Kathryn D. *Staying on Top When Your World Turns Upside Down*. New York: Viking Penguin, 1990.

Hudnut, Robert K. *Meeting God in the Darkness*. Ventura, Calif.: Regal Books, 1989.

Leman, Kevin. *How to Keep Your Family Together When the World Is Falling Apart*. New York: Delacorte Press, 1992.

Minar, Barbra Goodyear. *Close Connections: Creatively Loving Those Nearest You*. Wheaton, Ill.: Victor Books, 1992.

Ogilvie, Lloyd John. *God's Transforming Love*. Ventura, Calif.: Regal Books, 1988.

Phillips, Bob. *The Delicate Art of Dancing with Porcupines*. Ventura, Calif.: Regal Books, 1989.

Potash, Marlin S. *Hidden Agendas*. New York: Delacorte Press, 1990.

Notes

Notes

Notes

Notes

Notes

Notes

To place an order
or receive a **FREE**
catalog call toll free

(800) 328-3330